Awakening

Other Titles by Anthony de Mello

Awareness

The Heart of the Enlightened

One Minute Wisdom

Sadhana

The Song of the Bird

Taking Flight

The Way to Love

Wellsprings

Image Books

Doubleday

New York   London   Toronto

Sydney   Auckland

Awakening

*Conversations with
the Master*

Anthony de Mello

AN IMAGE BOOK
PUBLISHED BY DOUBLEDAY
a division of Random House, Inc.

IMAGE, DOUBLEDAY, and the portrayal of a deer
drinking from a stream are registered trademarks of
Random House, Inc.

Book design by Dana Leigh Treglia

Original English edition, *One Minute Wisdom* © 1992 by
Gujarat Sahitya Prakash, Anand, India. Previous North
American editions, *One Minute Wisdom* © 1992 and *More
One Minute Nonsense* © 1993 and *Awakening: Conversations
with the Master* © 1998 by Loyola Press.

The Library of Congress has cataloged the 1998 Loyola Press
edition as follows:

De Mello, Anthony, 1931–
Awakening : conversations with the Master / by Anthony
de Mello. — North American ed.
p. cm.
Rev. ed. of: One minute nonsense, 1992.
1. Meditations. I. De Mello, Anthony, 1931– One minute
nonsense. II. Title.
BX2182.2.D3875 1998
242—dc21 98-18327
CIP

ISBN 978-0-385-50995-4

First Image Books Edition

146122990

Who Is the Master?

The Master in these tales is not a single person. He is a Hindu guru, a Zen roshi, a Taoist sage, a Jewish rabbi, a Christian monk, a Sufi mystic. He is Lao Tzu and Socrates, Buddha and Jesus, Zarathustra and Muhammad. His teaching is found in the seventh century B.C. and the twentieth century A.D. His wisdom belongs to East and West alike. Do his historical antecedents really matter? History, after all, is the record of appearances, not Reality; of doctrines, not of Silence.

You will probably find the Master's language baffling, exasperating, even downright meaningless. This, alas, is not an easy book! It was written, not to instruct, but to Awaken. . . .

So explained Anthony de Mello, S.J., in the introduction to these stories, found among his papers after his death in 1987.

The masterful conversations and encounters are written by Fr. de Mello, himself a Master—a spiritually wise man intent on listening to the voice that speaks deep within the human heart, intent on sharing the "Silent Teaching" with those who have ears to hear it.

He continued, "Concealed within the pages (not in the printed words, not even in the tales, but in its spirit, its mood, its atmosphere) is a Wisdom that cannot be conveyed in human speech."

Of course the conversations *are* presented in human speech. The Master's wisdom is sometimes biting: "To be wronged is *nothing* unless you insist on remembering it." Sometimes cryptic: "May the peace of God disturb you always!" Often witty: "It isn't falling in (the river) that causes you to drown; it's staying in."

De Mello further explained:

As you read the printed page and struggle within the Master's cryptic language, it is possible that you will unwittingly chance upon the Silent Teaching that lurks within the book, and be Awakened—and transformed. This is what Wisdom means: to be changed without the slightest effort on your part, to be transformed, believe it or not, merely by waking to the reality that is not words, that lies beyond the reach of words.

If you are fortunate enough to be Awakened thus, you will know why the finest language is the one that is not spoken, the finest action is the one that is not done, and the finest change is the one that is not willed.

Fr. de Mello's spiritual leadership, first to young Jesuits in Bombay, India, bridged the traditions of East and West, transcended ideologies. Founder of the famed Sadhana Institute of Pastoral Counseling and Spirituality, de Mello gave retreats and offered spiritual direction and counseling that drew seekers to his challenging teaching. His reading and television audience grew in number and devotion. When he died suddenly in June 1987— only fifty-five years old—he was mourned around the world by friends, students, and readers who had found inspiration in his masterful ways. Not so much giving answers as asking questions that went to the heart of the matter.

De Mello left behind this manuscript of short, pithy encounters with the Master. He warned that they should be read "in tiny doses—one or two at a time. An overdose will lower their potency."

He also warned that on first reading some might be considered "nonsense." To make his point, he couldn't resist writing one exemplary moment with the Master:

> *"The man talks nonsense," said a visitor after hearing the Master speak.*
>
> *Said a disciple, "You would talk nonsense too if you were trying to express the inexpressible."*
>
> *When the visitor checked this out with the Master himself, this is the reply he got: "No one is exempt from talking nonsense. The great misfortune is to do it solemnly."*

Whether you already appreciate de Mello's work or are just browsing, looking for a daily nudge toward your own awakening, read on. Take the plunge. Open your eyes, your ears, your heart to the Master and his word.

1

Someone asked the Master the meaning of the phrase "The Enlightened person travels without moving."

Said the Master, "Sit at your window each day and observe the ever-changing scenery in your backyard as the earth carries you through its annual trip around the sun."

2

Said a disciple to a newcomer at the monastery, "I must warn you that you will not understand a word of what the Master says if you do not have the proper disposition."

"What is the proper disposition?"

"Be like a student eager to learn a foreign language. The words he speaks sound familiar, but don't be taken in; they have an altogether foreign meaning."

3

"A good way to discover your shortcomings," said the Master, "is to observe what irritates you in others."

He once told how his wife had placed a candy box on the kitchen shelf only to find, an hour later, that the box felt light. The whole bottom layer was gone, each piece neatly dropped into a paper bag that sat atop the new cook's belongings. Not willing to cause embarrassment, the Master's kindhearted wife merely replaced the candy and kept it in a cupboard out of temptation's way.

After dinner the cook announced she was leaving the job that very night.

"Why? What's the matter?" asked the Master.

"I won't work for people who steal back."

4

Next day the Master followed this up with the story of the burglar who found this sign on the door of the safe he was about to blow: "Please do not use dynamite. This safe is not locked. Just turn the knob."

The instant the thief turned the knob, a sandbag fell on him, floodlights came on, and sirens woke the entire neighborhood.

The Master visited the man in prison and found him bitter. "How am I ever going to trust another human being again?" he asked.

5

When a guest volunteered to do the dishes after dinner, the Master said, "Are you sure you know how to do dishes?"

The man protested that he had done them all his life. Said the Master, "Ah, I have no doubt of your ability to make dishes clean. I only doubt your ability to wash them."

6

This is the explanation the Master gave his disciples: "There are two ways to wash dishes: One is to wash them in order to make them clean; the other is to wash them in order to wash them."

That was still far from clear, so he added, "The first action is dead, because while your body does the dishes your mind is fixed on the goal of cleaning them; the second is alive, because your mind is where your body is."

7

"Enlightenment," said the Master, "means knowing precisely where you are at any given moment—not an easy task at all!"

And he told of a popular friend of his who was, even in his late eighties, invited to dozens of functions. Once he was spotted at a party and asked how many he was attending that night.

"Six," said the elderly gentleman, carefully examining his little notebook.

"What are you doing? Seeing where you are to go next?" they asked him.

"No," said the dynamic fellow. "Finding out where I am now."

8

The Master was allergic to ideologies.

"In a war of ideas," he said, "it is people who are the casualties."

Later he elaborated, "People kill for money or for power. But the most ruthless murderers are those who kill for their ideas."

9

It was lecture time and the Master said, "The genius of a composer is found in the notes of his music; but analyzing the notes will not reveal his genius. The poet's greatness is contained in his words; yet the study of his words will not disclose his inspiration. God reveals himself in creation; but scrutinize creation as minutely as you wish, you will not find God, any more than you will find the soul through the careful examination of your body."

At question time someone asked, "How then shall we find God?"

"By looking at creation, not by analyzing it."

10

"And how is one to look at creation?" another questioner asked.

The Master explained, "A peasant sets out to find beauty in the sunset, but all he finds is sun and cloud and sky and earth's horizon till he understands that beauty is not a 'thing' but a special way of looking. You will seek for God in vain till you understand that God can't be seen as 'thing'; God needs a special way of looking, similar to that of little children whose sight is undistorted by prefabricated doctrines and beliefs."

11

The father of a disciple stormed into the lecture hall where the Master was holding forth.

Ignoring everyone present, the father yelled at his daughter, "You have abandoned a university career to sit at the feet of this fool! What has he taught you?"

She stood up, calmly drew her father outside, and said, "Being with him has taught me what no university ever could—not to fear you and not to be embarrassed by your disgraceful behavior."

12

"What does one need in order to be Enlightened?" asked the disciples.

Said the Master, "You must discover what it is that falls in the water and does not make a ripple; moves through the trees and does not make a sound; enters the field and does not stir a single blade of grass."

After weeks of fruitless pondering, the disciples said, "What is this thing?"

"Thing?" said the Master. "But it isn't a thing at all."

"So it is nothing?"

"You might say so."

"Then how are we to search for it?"

"Did I tell you to search for it? It can be found but never searched for. Seek and you will miss."

13

The Master overheard an actress discoursing on horoscopes at dinnertime.

He leaned over and said, "You don't believe in astrology, do you?"

"Well," the actress replied, "I believe in everything a little bit."

14

Someone asked the Master if he believed in luck.

"Certainly," he replied with a twinkle in his eye. "How else can one explain the success of people one does not like?"

15

When asked how Scripture is to be used, the Master told of the time he was a schoolteacher and set the students this question: "How would you determine the height of a building by means of an aneroid barometer?"

One bright young student replied, "I would lower the barometer on a string and measure the string."

"Resourceful in his ignorance," the Master said.

Then he added, "Such is the resourcefulness and the ignorance of those who use their brains to understand Scripture, which can as well be 'understood' by the brain as can a sunset or the ocean or the murmur of the night wind in the trees."

16

A social worker poured out her woes to the Master. How much good she would be able to do for the poor if she did not have to spend so much time and energy protecting herself and her work from slander and misunderstandings.

The Master listened attentively, then responded in a single sentence: "No one throws stones at barren trees."

17

The Master was unsparing of those who wallowed in self-pity or resentment.

"To be wronged," he said, "is *nothing* unless you insist on remembering it."

18

"People don't want to give up their jealousies and anxieties, their resentment and guilt, because these negative emotions provide them with their 'kicks,' the feeling of being alive," said the Master.

And he illustrated his point with this story:

The local postman took a shortcut through a meadow on his bicycle. Midway across, a bull spied him and gave chase. The poor fellow barely made it to the fence.

"Nearly got you, didn't he?" said the Master, who had watched the scene.

"Yes," said the old man, puffing. "Nearly gets me every time."

19

A scientist came to protest that the Master's contempt for concepts as opposed to "conceptless knowledge" was unfair to science.

The Master was at pains to explain that he was a friend of science. "But," he said, "your knowledge of your wife had better go beyond the concept knowledge of science!"

20

Later, when talking to his disciples, the Master was more forceful. "Concepts define," he said. "To define is to destroy. Concepts dissect Reality. And what you dissect you kill."

"Are concepts then quite useless?"

"No. Dissect a rose and you will have valuable information—and no knowledge whatsoever—of the rose. Become a scholar and you will have much information—but no knowledge whatsoever—of Reality."

21

The Master claimed that the world most people see is not the world of Reality, but a world their head creates.

When a scholar came to dispute this, the Master set two sticks on the floor in the form of the letter T and asked, "What do you see here?"

"The letter T," said the scholar.

"Just as I thought," said the Master. "There's no such thing as a letter T; that's a symbol in your head. What you have here is two broken branches in the form of sticks."

22

"Name one practical, down-to-earth effect of spirituality," said the skeptic, who was ready for an argument.

"Here's one," said the Master. "When someone offends you, you can raise your spirits to heights where offenses cannot reach."

23

The Master told this parable:

A village blacksmith found an apprentice willing to work hard at low pay.

The smith immediately began his instructions to the lad. "When I take the metal out of the fire," he said, "I'll lay it on the anvil. When I nod my head, you hit it with the hammer."

The apprentice did precisely what he *thought* he was told. Next day he was the village blacksmith.

24

Later the Master explained the parable of the blacksmith's apprentice.

"When you speak about Reality," he said, "you are attempting to put the inexpressible into words, so your words are certain to be misunderstood. Thus people who read that expression of Reality called the Scriptures become stupid and cruel, for they follow, not their common sense, but what they think their Scriptures say."

25

To a disciple who was terrified about making mistakes, the Master said, "Those who make no mistakes are making the biggest mistake of all. They are attempting nothing new."

26

"Tell me," said the atheist, "is there really a God?"

Said the Master, "If you want me to be perfectly honest with you, I will not answer."

27

Later the disciples demanded to know why the Master had not answered the question "Is there a God?"

"Because his question is unanswerable," said the Master.

"So you are an atheist?"

"Certainly not. The atheist makes the mistake of denying that of which nothing may be said."

After pausing to let that sink in, he added, "And the theist makes the mistake of affirming it."

28

"What is the secret of your serenity?"

Said the Master, "Wholehearted cooperation with the inevitable."

29

The Master and a disciple came upon a blind man sitting on the sidewalk, begging.

Said the Master, "Give the man an alms."

The disciple dropped a coin in the beggar's hat.

Said the Master, "You should have touched your hat as a mark of respect."

"Why?" asked the disciple.

"One always should when one gives an alms."

"But the man was blind."

"You never know," said the Master. "He may have been a fraud."

30

Said the tourist, "The people of your country are poor. But they never seem preoccupied."

Said the Master, "That is because they never look at the clock."

31

Some of the disciples were on an excursion high up on a snow-clad mountain. Everywhere a cosmic silence prevailed. They were curious to find out if there were any sounds at night, so they pressed the record button on a tape recorder, left it at the entrance of their tent, and went to sleep.

They got back to the monastery and replayed the tape. Not a sound; total, unsullied silence.

The Master, who was listening to the tape, broke in, saying, "Don't you hear it?"

"Hear what?"

"The harmony of galaxies in motion," said the Master.

The disciples looked at one another in wonder.

32

The monastery was getting crowded, and a larger building was needed. So a merchant wrote out a check for a million dollars and placed it before the Master, who picked it up and said, "Very well. I shall accept it."

The merchant was dissatisfied. That was a large sum of money, and the Master hadn't even thanked him.

"There are a million dollars in that check," he said.

"Yes, so I have observed."

"Even if I am a wealthy man, a million dollars is a lot of money."

"Do you want me to thank you for it?"

"You ought to."

"Why should I? The giver should be thankful," said the Master.

33

The Master's attitude to social service was perplexing. At times, he was all for it. At others, he seemed indifferent.

The explanations he sometimes gave for this inconsistency were just as enigmatic:

"The one who wishes to do good must knock at the gate.

"For the one who loves, the gate is always open."

34

A disciple had to rush back home when he got news that his house had burned down.

He was an old man, and everyone commiserated with him. All that the Master said to him was, "This will make dying easier."

35

"The Enlightened person," said the Master, "is one who sees that everything in the world is perfect exactly as it is."

"What about the gardener?" someone asked. "Is he perfect too?"

The monastery gardener was a hunchback.

"For what he is meant to be in life," said the Master, "the gardener is a perfect hunchback."

36

The disciples were distressed to see the Master's teachings ridiculed in a national magazine.

The Master was unperturbed. "Could anything be really true," he said, "if no one laughed at it?"

37

The idea that everything in the world is perfect was more than the disciples could accept. So the Master put it in concepts that were more within their grasp.

"God weaves perfect designs with the threads of our lives," he said. "Even with our sins. We can't see this because we're looking at the reverse side of the tapestry."

38

The Master elaborated with another example: "What some people take for a shiny stone, the jeweler recognizes as a diamond."

39

In his younger days, the Master had been a political activist and had led a protest march against the government. Thousands of people had left their homes and jobs to join the agitation.

The march had hardly begun when he called the whole thing off. "You simply cannot do this," said his followers. "The march has been planned for months and has cost the people dearly. They will accuse you of being inconsistent."

The Master was unmoved. "My commitment is not to consistency," he said, "but to the truth."

40

One reason people are so unhappy is that they think there is nothing they cannot change.

The Master especially enjoyed the story of the man who said to the shopkeeper, "This radio you sold me is excellent for quality of sound, but I want it exchanged for one that has better programs."

41

"What is it you seek?"

"Peace," said the visitor.

"To those who seek to protect their ego, true peace only brings disturbance."

And to a religious group that came to gawk at him and ask for a blessing, he said with a roguish smile, "May the peace of God disturb you always!"

42

Back from a bus trip, the Master told of an experience he thought was a parable on life:

During a brief stop, he walked to a neat-looking lunch counter. There were delicious soups and hot curries.

He ordered soup.

"Are you from the bus?" asked the attendant.

The Master nodded yes.

"No soup," she said.

"Hot curry with steamed rice?" asked the Master, puzzled.

"Not if you're on the bus. You can have sandwiches. It took me all morning to prepare the soups and curries, and you have been given only ten minutes to eat. I won't let you eat food that you don't have the time to relish."

43

There was nothing pompous about the Master. Wild, hilarious laughter prevailed each time he spoke, to the dismay of those who were solemn about their spirituality—and themselves.

Said one disillusioned visitor, "The man's a clown!"

"No, no," said a disciple. "You've missed the point: A clown gets you to laugh at him; the Master gets you to laugh at yourself."

44

"How does one learn to trust in Providence?"

"Trusting in Providence," said the Master, "is like walking into an expensive restaurant without a cent in your pocket and eating dozens of oysters in the hope of finding a pearl to pay the bill!"

45

The Master once offered a banana to an awestruck visitor who so venerated the gift that he hardly knew what to do with it.

When the Master was told of this, he said characteristically, "Tell the silly ass to eat it."

46

It scandalized the disciples that the Master had such little use for worship.

"Find yourself an object of veneration," he used to say, "and you piously distract yourself from what is essential—awareness that leads to love."

And in self-defense, he would cite Jesus' scorn of those who cried, "Lord! Lord!" and were quite unaware of the evil they were doing.

47

Said a recently arrived disciple to one with more experience, "Why do I seem to gain so little from living with the Master?"

"Could it be because you came to learn spirituality from him?"

"What, may I ask, did you come for?"

"To see him fasten his sandal straps!"

48

It was a joy to behold the Master perform the simplest acts—sit or walk or drink a cup of tea or drive away a fly. There was a grace in all he did that made him seem in harmony with nature, as though his actions were produced not by him but by the universe.

Once when the Master received a parcel, the disciples, spellbound, watched him reverently untie the string, unfold the paper, and lift the contents as though the parcel were a living creature.

49

A religious woman told the Master she had been to confession that morning.

"I can't imagine you committing a grave sin," said the Master. "What did you confess?"

"Well, I was too lazy to go to Mass one Sunday, and I swore at the gardener once. And I once drove my mother-in-law out of the house for a whole week."

"But that happened five years ago, didn't it? Surely you've been to confession since then."

"Yes, I have. But I confess it every time. I like to remember it."

50

"Someday you will understand that you are seeking what you already have," said the Master to an intense disciple.

"Then why do I not see it now?"

"Because you are trying to."

"Must I then make no efforts?"

"If you relax and give it time, it will make itself known."

51

For people who practiced virtue in order to get God's friendship or favor, the Master had this to say:

A large crowd of people were taking part in a Cadillac-giveaway contest sponsored by a soap manufacturer.

They were asked, "Why do you like Heaven Scent soap?"

One woman replied honestly, "Because I'd love to own a Cadillac."

52

"I have been four months with you, and you have still not given me a method or technique."

"A method?" said the Master. "What on earth would you want a method for?"

"To attain inner freedom."

The Master roared with laughter. "You need great skill indeed to set yourself free by means of the trap called a method."

53

When a disciple complained that the Master's spirituality needed updating, the Master laughed aloud. Then he told the story of a student who said, "Haven't you any more recent books on anatomy? These are at least ten years old."

Said the bookseller, "Look, son, there have been no bones added to the human body in the last ten years."

"Neither," added the Master, "has there been any addition to human nature in the last ten thousand years."

54

The Master once proposed a riddle: "What do the artist and the musician have in common with the mystic?"

Everyone gave up.

"The realization that the finest speech does not come from the tongue," said the Master.

55

Rarely was the Master so eloquent as when he warned against the bewitching power of words.

"Beware of words," he said. "The moment you look away, they will take on a life of their own; they will dazzle, mesmerize, terrorize, lead you astray from the reality they represent, lead you to believe they are real.

"The world you see is not the kingdom seen by children, but a fragmented world, broken into a thousand pieces by the word. It is as if each ocean wave were seen to be distinct and separate from the body of the ocean."

56

The Master continued, "When words and thoughts are silenced, the universe blossoms forth—real and whole and one—and words become what they were always meant to be: the score, not the music; the menu, not the food; the signpost, not the journey's end."

57

The Master was walking down a street when a man rushed out of a doorway and the two collided with great force.

The man was beside himself with rage and exploded into abusive language. The Master made a little bow, smiled pleasantly, and said, "My friend, I do not know which of us is responsible for this encounter, but I am not inclined to waste time investigating. If I ran into you, I beg your pardon; if you ran into me, don't mention it."

Then, with another bow, he walked away.

58

To a painter the Master said, "To be successful, every painter must invest hours in unremitting toil and effort.

"To some it will be given to let go of the ego as they paint. When this happens, a masterpiece is born."

Later a disciple asked, "Who is a master?"

The Master replied, "Anyone to whom it is given to let go of the ego. Such a person's life is then a masterpiece."

59

The Master always taught that truth was right before his disciples' eyes. The reason they did not see it was their lack of perspective.

Once he took a disciple on a mountain trip. When they were halfway up the mountain, the man glared at the underbrush and complained, "Where's the beautiful scenery you are always talking about?"

The Master grinned. "You're standing on top of it, as you will see when we reach the peak."

60

"Where shall I find a worthy master when I get back to my country?"

"There isn't a single moment when you are without one."

The disciple was confused.

"Simply watching your reaction to everything—a bird, a leaf, a tear, a smile—makes everything your master."

61

The Master was certainly not a stickler for etiquette, but there was always a natural courtesy and grace in his dealings with others.

A young disciple was once very rude to a traffic policeman as the disciple drove the Master home one night. In self-defense, the disciple said, "I'd rather be myself and let people know exactly how I feel. Politeness is nothing but a lot of hot air."

"True enough," said the Master pleasantly. "But that's what we have in our automobile tires, and see how it eases the bumps."

62

Once when the Master spoke of the hypnotic power of words, someone from the back of the room shouted, "You're talking non-sense! If I say, 'God, God, God,' will that make me divine? And if I say, 'Sin, sin, sin,' will it make me evil?"

"Sit down, you bastard!" said the Master.

The man became so livid that it took him some time to recover his speech. Then he screamed a torrent of abuse at the Master.

The Master, looking contrite, said, "Pardon me, sir, I was carried away. I truly apologize for my unpardonable lapse."

The man calmed down immediately.

"Well, there you have your answer. All it took was a word to give you a fit and another to sedate you," said the Master.

63

The governor resigned his exalted office and came to the Master demanding to be taught.

"What is it you wish me to teach you?" said the Master.

"Wisdom," was the reply.

"Ah, my friend! How gladly would I do that were it not for one major obstacle."

"What?"

"Wisdom can't be taught."

"So there's nothing I can learn here."

"Wisdom can be learned. But it can't be taught."

64

Attachment distorts our perception. This was a frequent theme of the Master's discourses.

The disciples were once entertained by a perfect example of this when they heard the Master ask a mother, "How is your daughter?"

"My darling daughter! How fortunate she is! She has such a wonderful husband! He has given her a car, all the jewelry she wants, servants galore. He serves her breakfast in bed, and she doesn't get up till noon. What a prince of a man!"

"And your son?"

"Oh, the poor boy! What a vixen he has married! He has given her a car, all the jewelry she wants, and an army of servants. And she stays in bed till noon! Won't even get up to give him his breakfast!"

65

Everyone was talking about the religious man who committed suicide.

While no one in the monastery approved of the man's action, some said they admired his faith.

"Faith?" said the Master.

"He had the courage of his convictions, didn't he?"

"That was fanaticism, not faith. Faith demands a greater courage still: to reexamine one's convictions and reject them if they do not fit the facts."

66

When the Master was a boy at school, a classmate treated him with persistent cruelty.

Now, older and contrite, the former classmate came to the monastery and was received with open arms.

One day he brought up the subject of his former cruelty, but the Master seemed not to recall it.

Said the visitor, "Don't you remember?"

Said the Master, "I distinctly remember forgetting it!" And they both melted in innocent laughter.

67

A mother asked when she should begin the education of her child.

"How old is she?" asked the Master.

"She's five."

"Five! Hurry home! You're five years late already."

68

When the Master heard that a neighboring forest had been devastated by fire, he mobilized all his disciples. "We must replant the cedars," he said.

"The cedars?" exclaimed an incredulous disciple. "But they take two thousand years to grow!"

"In that case," said the Master, "there is not a minute to lose. We must set out at once."

69

A friend said to a university student, "What do you go to the Master for? Will he help you earn a living?"

"No, but thanks to him I will know what to do with the living when I earn one."

70

"Your religious leaders are just as blind and confused as you are," said the Master. "When confronted with life's problems, all they come up with is answers from a book. But life is too large to fit into any book."

71

Later the Master told of the thug who said, "This is a holdup! Give me your money or else."

"Or else what?"

"Don't confuse me. This is my first job."

72

"How does the Master explain the evil in the world?" asked a visitor.

One disciple replied, "He doesn't explain it. He's too busy doing something about it."

73

Another disciple said, "People are forever fighting the world or bored with it. The Master is enchanted with what he sees as stupendous, awesome, unfathomable."

74

The preacher was widely acclaimed for his eloquence. But he confessed to his friends that his eloquent speech never had quite the effect of the Master's unadorned pronouncements.

After living with the Master for a week, he knew exactly why.

"When he speaks," said the preacher, "his speech embodies silence. My speech, alas, embodies thought."

75

The Master had what amounted to a veneration for the human body. When a disciple referred to it as an "earthen vessel," the Master rapturously quoted the poet Kabir:

"Within this earthen vessel are canyons and Himalayan mountains; the seven seas are here and a thousand million galaxies; and the music of the spheres and the source of waterfalls and rivers."

76

When the Master met a group of teachers, he spoke long and animatedly, for he had been a teacher himself. The trouble with teachers, he said, is that they keep forgetting that the goal of education is not learning but life.

And he told of the report card his little daughter got: "Meena is doing well in school. She would do much better if the pure joy of living did not impede her progress."

77

The Master told of the time he spotted a boy fishing in the river.

"Hello! Nice day for fishing!" he said to the boy.

"Yes," came the reply.

After a while the Master said, "Why aren't you in school today?"

"Well, sir, like you said, it's a nice day for fishing."

78

The Master loved to show how nature is shot through with holiness. He was once sitting in the garden when he exclaimed, "Look at that bright bluebird sitting on the branch of that tree springing up and down, up and down, filling the world with its melody, abandoning itself to unreserved delight because it has no notion of tomorrow."

79

"The law is an expression of God's holy will and as such must be honored and loved," said the preacher piously.

"Rubbish," said the Master. "The law is a necessary evil and as such must be cut down to the barest minimum. Show me a lover of the law, and I will show you a mutton-headed tyrant."

80

The Master illustrated this point. He told of his sister who got tired of pushing her daughter's baby carriage, so she had a motor put on it.

Then the police stepped into the picture. They said that since the powered carriage could travel three miles an hour, it had to be classified as a self-propelled vehicle. Therefore the mother would have to get a license, plates, lights, brakes, and, to crown it all, a driver's license!

81

The Master went on to tell of the astronaut who returned from a five-hundred-orbit voyage around the earth. When asked how he felt, he said, "Exhausted! Think how many times I had to say the morning, noon, evening, and night prayers prescribed by my religion!"

82

For the Master, all rules, no matter how sacred, had a purely functional value and had to yield to Reality, which alone was law supreme.

When his teenage daughter, following the fashion, wanted to wear an off-the-shoulder dress, her mother felt she wasn't old enough for that sort of gown. A heated argument ensued for days.

When the Master was finally appealed to, he said, "Let her try one on. If it stays up, she's old enough to wear it."

83

A religious writer asked for a word of wisdom.

Said the Master, "Some people write to make a living; others to share their insights or raise questions that will haunt their readers; others yet to understand their very souls.

"None of these will last. That distinction belongs to those who write only because if they did not they would burst."

As an afterthought he added, "These writers give expression to the divine—no matter *what* they write about."

84

When asked what Enlightenment felt like, the Master said, "It is like going into the wilderness and suddenly feeling that you are being watched."

"By whom?"

"By rocks and trees and mountains."

"An eerie feeling."

"No, a comforting one. But because it is unfamiliar, one feels the urge to rush back to the commonplace world of people—their noise, their words, their laughter—which has cut us off from nature and Reality."

85

A disciple was prone to fits of prolonged depression. "My doctor insists I take medication to keep my depression at bay," he said.

"Well, then, why don't you?" said the Master.

"Because it might damage my liver and shorten my life."

Said the Master, "Would you rather have a healthy liver than a happy mood? One year of life is worth more than twenty years of hibernation."

Later he said to his disciples, "It is with life as with a tale—what matters is not how long it is but how good."

86

"Does it ever bring you joy to see the fruits of your endeavors?"

The Master replied, "How much joy does it give a tool to see what the hand has done?"

87

One day the Master said, "Good deeds done by the unconscious are superior to good deeds that are willed."

This produced a flurry of questions that the Master nimbly sidestepped as he always did when he judged that the time to answer them had not arrived.

One day everyone went to the performance of a world-famous pianist. Said the Master in a whisper to his neighbor, "The movement of that woman's fingers over the keyboard is something that cannot be willed. Work of that quality must be left to the unconscious."

88

A visitor to the monastery was particularly struck by what he called the Master's radiance. One day when he happened to meet an old friend of the Master's, the visitor asked if there was any explanation for it.

Said the friend, "Let me put it this way: Life is a mystery. Death is the key that unlocks it. The moment you turn the key, you disappear into the mystery forever."

"Do we have to wait for death before we turn the key?" said the visitor.

"No! You could turn it now—through silence—and dissolve into the mystery. Then you too would become radiant like the Master."

89

Enthralled at hearing the Master chant Sanskrit verses in a melodious voice, a Sanskrit scholar said, "I have always known that there is no language on earth like Sanskrit for the expression of things divine."

"Don't be an ass," said the Master. "The language of the divine isn't Sanskrit. It is silence."

90

The Master was amused at the kind of phony self-deprecation that passes for humility. Here is a parable he told his disciples:

A priest and a sexton went to a church to pray. The priest began to beat his breast and, carried away, cried out, "I am the lowliest of men, Lord, unworthy of your grace! I am a void, a nothing. Have mercy on me."

Not far from the priest was the sexton who, in an outburst of fervor, also beat his breast and cried, "Have mercy, Lord! I'm a sinner, a nothing."

The priest turned round haughtily. "Ha!" he said. "Look who's claiming to be nothing!"

91

"Why . . . why . . . why?" demanded the disciple when, to his astonishment, the Master insisted on his leaving the monastery forthwith barely twenty-four hours after he had been welcomed.

"Because you do not need a master. I can show you the way, but only you can do the walking. I can point to the water, but you alone can do the drinking. Why waste your time here gazing starry-eyed at me? You know the way. Walk! The water is right in front of you. Drink!"

92

A group of pilgrims asked for a word of wisdom.

The Master, who was quick to spot people in the religion business, said, "Understand that you are not truly spiritual at all."

Offended, they demanded an explanation. The Master told this tale:

A rabbit and a lion once walked into a restaurant. People in the restaurant couldn't believe what they were seeing.

Said the rabbit to the waiter, "Lettuce, please. No dressing."

"What about your friend?" asked the waiter. "What shall I bring him?"

"Nothing."

"You mean the lion isn't hungry?"

The rabbit looked the waiter in the eye and said, "If he were a lion, do you think he would be sitting here? He's a sham!"

93

Said a curious disciple, "Give us a sign to know when one is Enlightened."

Said the Master, "Here's one: You find yourself asking, 'Is it I who am crazy, or is it everyone else?' "

94

In respect to preachers and priests, the Master always urged people to look for competence, not claims.

Two tourists were approaching Honolulu, he said, and got into an argument about the correct pronunciation of *Hawaii*. One said it was "Ha*w*aii." The other affirmed it was "Ha*v*aii."

The first thing they did on landing was approach a local resident. "Aloha! How do you people pronounce the name of the island: 'Ha*w*aii' or 'Ha*v*aii'?"

"Ha*v*aii."

"Thank you."

"A very varm velcome to both of you," said the local.

95

"What is the work of a master?" asked a solemn-faced visitor.

"To teach people to laugh," said the Master gravely.

96

Another time the Master declared, "When you are able to laugh in the face of life, you become sovereign of the world—just like the person who is prepared to die."

97

"How does one recognize Enlightenment?"

"By the fact that, having seen evil as evil, the Enlightened person cannot do it," said the Master.

"And cannot be tempted either," he added. "All the others are frauds."

98

Then the Master told the story of a smuggler who, fearing police raids, went to a very holy monk to beg him to hide some contraband in his monastery. Given the monk's reputation for holiness, no one would suspect him.

The monk grew indignant and demanded that the man leave the monastery at once.

"I'll give you a hundred thousand dollars for your charities," said the smuggler.

The monk hesitated, ever so slightly, before saying no.

"Two hundred thousand." Still the monk refused.

"Five hundred thousand." The monk took hold of a stick and yelled, "Get out this minute. You're getting too close to my price."

99

"Do you believe in life after death?" a disciple asked at the end of a long conversation about the future.

"Strange that you should be so stuck to that topic!" said the Master.

"Why would you think it strange?"

"Here you have this glorious April day in front of you," said the Master, pointing to the window. "You're like a child who refuses to eat today because he does not know what tomorrow will bring. You're starving. Eat your daily bread!"

100

"I am affluent, but miserable. Why?"

"Because you spend too much time making money and too little making love," said the Master.

1○1

"Only a foolish person would hesitate to give up everything in exchange for truth," said the Master.

And he told them the following parable:

During an oil boom in a small country town, landowners eagerly sold every square foot of land to the oil companies in exchange for fortunes.

One old lady refused to sell at any price.

The offers rose to astronomical figures till one oil company declared it was ready to give her any price she named. Still she held out, and a friend demanded to know why.

"Don't you see that if I sell, I'll lose my only source of income?" the old lady explained.

102

The Master taught that change, even change for the good, always carries side effects that have to be carefully examined before change is sought. The invention of gunpowder brought protection from wild beasts—and modern warfare. The automobile brought speed—and air pollution. Modern technology saves lives—and makes our bodies flabby.

103

Later the Master told this story:

There was once a man who had a golden belly button that caused him endless embarrassment, for each time he took a shower or swim, he was the butt of people's jokes. He prayed and prayed to have the belly button changed. Then one night he dreamt that an angel unscrewed it and, leaving it on a table, disappeared.

On awakening in the morning, he saw the dream was true. There on the table lay the shiny golden belly button. The man jumped up in ecstasy—and his real belly button fell off!

104

One day a philosopher asked, "What is the purpose of creation?"

"Lovemaking," said the Master.

Later, to his disciples, he said, "Before creation, love was. After creation, love is made. When love is consummated, creation will cease to be, and love will be forever."

105

One day when the talk turned to modern technology, the Master told of a friend of his who wanted to encourage a taste for music in his children. So he bought them a piano.

When he got home that evening, he found them contemplating the piano in puzzlement. "How," they asked, "do you plug it in?"

106

As a young man, the Master had done a lot of traveling around the world. He was at the port of Shanghai, China, once when he heard loud screaming next to his boat. Looking out, he saw a man leaning over the side of a nearby junk hanging on to the long hair of another man who was thrashing about in the water.

The man in the junk would push the other under the water, then yank him up again. The two would then argue wildly for a minute or so before the dunking was repeated.

The Master rang for the cabin boy and asked what the quarrel was about. The boy listened for a moment, laughed, and said, "Nothing, sir. Man in boat want sixty yuan to not drown other man. Man in water say no, only forty yuan."

After the disciples laughed at the story, the Master said, "Is there a single one of you who isn't bargaining about the only life there is?" All of them were silent.

107

"Who is a happy person?"

"One who has no resources and no hopes—and doesn't desire any," said the Master.

108

The Master never let a statement about God go unchallenged. All God statements were poetic or symbolic expressions of the unknowable; people, however, foolishly took them as literal descriptions of the divine.

When the preacher said, "This much I know of God, that he is wise and good," the Master countered with, "Then why does God stand by helplessly in the face of evil?"

Said the preacher, "How should I know? What do you think I am, a mystic?"

109

Later the Master regaled his disciples with this Jewish tale:

Two men sat sipping tea in silence. After a while one said, "Life is like a bowl of lukewarm soup."

"A bowl of lukewarm soup?" asked the other. "Why?"

"How should I know? What do you think I am, a philosopher?"

110

The Master once referred to the Hindu notion that all creation is *leela*—God's play—and that the universe is God's playground. The aim of spirituality, he claimed, is to make all life play.

This seemed too frivolous for a puritanical visitor. "Is there no room then for work?" he asked the Master.

"Of course there is. But work becomes spiritual only when it is transformed into play."

111

"My temple priest tells me that the temple is the only place for me to worship in. What do you say?"

"Your temple priest isn't the best person to consult on these matters," said the Master.

"But he's the expert, isn't he?"

In reply, the Master told of an experience he had in a foreign country as he glanced through two guidebooks he had brought. His guide frowned at the guidebooks, pointed to one of them, and said, "This one very bad guidebook. Other one better."

"Why? Does this one have more information?"

The guide shook his head. "This book say give guide five dollar. That one say give guide fifty cent."

112

"One reason you join a religious organization is the chance it offers you to dodge religion with a clear conscience," said the Master.

And he told of a conversation he had with a disciple engaged to a traveling salesman:

"Is he good-looking?" asked the Master.

"Well, he certainly wouldn't stand out in a crowd."

"Does he have money?"

"If he does, he won't spend it."

"Does he have any bad habits?"

"He certainly smokes and drinks a lot more than is good for him."

"I don't understand you. If you can't find anything good to say about him, why marry him?"

"Well, he's mostly on the road and away from home. That way I have the satisfaction of being married without the burden of a husband."

113

The Master hardly ever spoke of spiritual topics. He was content to eat and work and play with the disciples and join with them in conversation on a thousand different topics ranging from the political situation of the country to the latest barroom joke.

A visitor once said, "How can the man teach you when he'd rather tell a joke than speak of God?"

Said a disciple, "There are other ways of teaching than through the use of words."

114

Someone asked the Master what "disinterested action" meant.

He replied, "Action that is loved and done for its own sake, not for any approval or profit or gain."

115

Then the Master told of a man who was hired by a researcher, taken to a backyard, and given an axe.

"Do you see that log lying there? Well, I want you to go through the motions of chopping it—only you must use the reverse side of the axe, not the blade. You'll get a hundred dollars an hour for that."

The man thought the researcher was crazy, but the pay seemed excellent, so he started to work.

Two hours later he told the researcher that he was quitting.

"What's the matter? Don't you like the pay you're getting? I'll double your wages!"

"No, thank you," said the man. "The pay is fine. But when I chop wood, I've got to see the chips fly!"

116

To a couple anxious about the upbringing of their children, the Master quoted a rabbinical saying:

"Do not limit your children to your own learning, for they have been born in another age."

117

"Could action lead to Enlightenment?" the Master was asked.

"Only action leads to Enlightenment," was his reply. "But it must be nonprofit action, done for its own sake."

118

The Master explained how he once sat in the stands with the little son of a soccer star who was playing a practice game. When the man shot a brilliant goal, everyone cheered. The kid wasn't impressed; he just sat there looking bored.

"What's the matter with you?" said the Master. "Didn't you see your father score that goal?"

"Yeah, he scored it all right today. But the match is on Friday. That's when the goals are needed."

The Master concluded, "Actions are valued if they help you score goals—not for themselves, alas."

119

"The principal reason why people are not happy is that they get a perverse satisfaction from their sufferings," said the Master.

He told how he was once traveling on the upper berth of a train at night. It was impossible to sleep because from the lower berth came the ceaseless moan of a woman. "Oh, how thirsty I am . . . God, how thirsty I am . . . !"

The Master finally crept down the ladder, filled two large paper cups with water, and handed them to the tormented woman.

"Lady, here. Water!"

"God bless you, sir. Thank you."

The Master climbed back into his berth, settled down comfortably, and was on the verge of falling into blissful slumber when from below came the lament "Oh, how thirsty I *was* . . . God, how thirsty I *was* . . . !"

120

The Master wasn't given to practices of devotion.

When questioned about it, he said, "A lamp loses its rays when set beside the sun; even the tallest temple looks so tiny at the foot of a Himalayan mountain."

121

When asked if he was ever discouraged by the little fruit his efforts seemed to yield, the Master told the story of a snail that started to climb a cherry tree one cold, windy day in late spring.

The sparrows on a neighboring tree had a good laugh at his expense. Then one flew over and said, "Hey, blockhead, don't you know there are no cherries on this tree?"

The little fellow did not stop but replied, "Well, there will be when I get there."

122

The Master loved a game of cards and once sat through an all-night air raid totally absorbed in playing poker with some of his disciples. When they stopped for drinks, the conversation turned to the subject of death.

"If I were to drop dead in the middle of this game, what would you do?" asked the Master.

"What would you wish us to do?"

"Two things. First, get the body out of the way."

"And the second?"

"Deal," said the Master.

123

"Why did you come to the Master?"

"Because my life was going nowhere, giving me nothing."

"So where's it going now?"

"Nowhere."

"And what's it giving you now?"

"Nothing."

"So what's the difference?"

"Now I'm going nowhere because there's nowhere to go; I'm getting nothing because there's nothing to desire."

124

To a man who spent years studying the law of his religion, the Master said, "It is love that is the key to the good life, not religion or the law."

Then he told of two Sunday school students who were sick of religious instructions, so one suggested they run away.

"Run away? But our fathers will get hold of us and thrash us."

"We'll hit them back."

"What? Hit your *father*? You must be out of your mind. Have you forgotten that God commands us to honor our father and mother?"

"True. OK, you hit my father and I'll hit yours."

125

The Master claimed that it made no sense at all to define oneself as Indian, Chinese, African, American, Hindu, Christian, or Muslim, for these are merely labels.

To a disciple who claimed he was Jewish first, last, and above all else, the Master said benignly, "Your conditioning is Jewish, not your identity."

"What's my identity?"

"Nothing," said the Master.

"You mean I am an emptiness and a void?" asked the incredulous disciple.

"Nothing that can be labeled," said the Master.

126

At the Master's birthday party, a disciple somewhat pointedly refused a glass of wine.

As he moved around the room, he happened to run into the Master, who gave him a wink and whispered, "You still have some interesting things to learn, my friend."

"What, for instance?"

"For instance, you could dye your prayer rug in wine, and it would still be soaked with God."

127

The Master enjoined not austerity but moderation. If one truly enjoyed things, he claimed, one would be spontaneously moderate.

Asked why he was so opposed to ascetical practices, he replied, "Because they produce pleasure haters who always become people haters—rigid and cruel."

"But lots of pleasure lovers are rigid and cruel."

"Not so. It is not pleasure they love, for they stuff themselves with it. What they love is the punishment they inflict on their bodies through excessive pleasure."

128

The Master taught mostly in parables and stories. Someone asked a disciple where the Master got them from.

"From God," was the reply. "When God means you to be a healer, God sends you patients; when God makes you a teacher, God sends you pupils; when God destines you to be a master, God sends you stories."

129

When asked about Jesus' injunction to his disciples to hate their parents, the Master said, "You will rarely find a greater enemy than a parent."

And he told of meeting a woman at the supermarket who was pushing a pram with two little boys in it.

"What cute kids you have," said the Master. "How old are they?"

"The doctor," said the woman, "is three, and the lawyer is two."

130

To those disciples who were naively confident that there was nothing they couldn't achieve if they went at it with a will, the Master would say, "The best things in life cannot be willed into being. You can will to put food in your mouth, but you cannot will an appetite. You can will to lie in bed, but you cannot will sleep. You can will to pay someone a compliment, but you cannot will admiration. You can will to tell a secret, but you cannot will trust. You can will an act of service, but you cannot will love."

131

"Each time you seek to change another," said the Master, "ask yourself this: What will be served by this change—my pride, my pleasure, or my profit?"

132

Then the Master told the following story:

A man was about to jump off a bridge when a policeman rushed up to him.

"No, no!" he cried. "Please don't do it. Why would a young fellow like you who hasn't even lived think of jumping into the water?"

"Because I'm sick of life."

"Now listen to me, please. If you jump into the river, I'll have to go in after you to save you. Right? Well, the water is freezing cold, and I've only just recovered from a bout of double pneumonia. Do you know what that means? I will die. I have a wife and four kids. Would you want to live with a thing like that on your conscience? No, of course not. So listen to me. Be good. Repent and God will forgive you. Go back home. And, in the privacy and quiet of your home, hang yourself."

133

Irritated by the Master's paradoxical language, a philosopher from Europe exclaimed, "I have heard it said that east of the Suez Canal two contradictory statements can be simultaneously true."

The Master enjoyed that one. "East of Suez," he said, "and one inch into Reality. That is why Reality is an unintelligible mystery."

134

There were no clocks in the monastery. When a businessman complained about the lack of punctuality, the Master said, "Ours is a cosmic punctuality, not a business punctuality."

This made no sense to the businessman, so the Master added, "Everything depends on your point of view. From the viewpoint of the forest, what is the loss of a leaf? From the viewpoint of the cosmos, what is the loss of your business schedule?"

135

"I thought that spirituality has nothing to do with politics," said a somewhat shocked disciple when she first became acquainted with the Master's political activities.

"That's because you have no idea what spirituality is all about," the Master replied.

Another day he called out to her and said, "You have no idea what politics is all about either."

136

"Why aren't more people Enlightened?"

"Because it isn't truth they seek, but their convenience," said the Master. He showed this by means of a Sufi tale:

A man in need of money sought to sell a rough carpet in the street. The first man to whom he showed it said, "This is a coarse carpet and very worn." And he bought it very cheaply.

A minute later, the buyer went around the corner and said to another man who happened along, "Here is a carpet soft as silk, sir. None like it."

Said a Sufi who had witnessed the scene, "Please, carpet man, put me into your magic box that can turn a rough carpet into a smooth one, a pebble into a precious stone."

"The magic box, of course," added the Master, "is called self-interest—the most effective tool in the world for turning truth into deception."

137

An art writer was giving a lecture at the monastery.

"Art is found in a museum," he said, "but beauty is found everywhere—in the air, on the ground, all over the place, free for the taking, with no name attached to it."

"Exactly like spirituality," said the Master the following day when he was alone with his disciples. "Its symbols are found in the museum called a temple, but its substance is everywhere, free for the taking, unrecognized, with no name attached to it."

138

The Master, fascinated as he was by modern technology, refused to call it progress.

True progress for him was "heart progress" and "happiness progress," not "brain progress" or "gadget progress."

"What do you think of modern civilization?" he was once asked by a reporter.

"I think that would be a very good idea," he said.

139

When talk of modern progress came up one day, the Master told of two visitors from a developing country.

He asked about the economic state of their people. One of the visitors took offense. "But, man," he said, "we're civilized. We even have a couple of ammunition factories!"

140

To a social worker the Master said, "I fear you are doing more harm than good."

"Why?"

"Because you stress only one of the two imperatives of justice."

"Namely?"

"The poor have a right to bread."

"What's the other one?"

"The poor have a right to beauty."

141

The Master's complaint against most social activists was this: What they sought was reform, not revolution.

"There was once a very wise and gentle king," he said, "who learned that there were a number of innocent persons in his state prison. So he decreed that another, more comfortable prison be constructed for the innocent."

142

The Master could be quite critical when he thought that criticism was in order.

But to everyone's surprise, he was never resented for his reprimands. When asked about this once, he said, "It depends on how one does it. Human beings are flowers—open and receptive to softly falling dew, closed to violent rain."

143

A disciple, in his reverence for the Master, looked upon him as God incarnate.

"Tell me, O Master," he said, "why you have come to this world."

"To teach fools like you to stop wasting their time worshiping masters."

144

When someone boasted of the economic and cultural achievements of his country, the Master was quite unimpressed. "Have all those achievements made the slightest change in the hearts of your countrymen?" he asked.

And the Master told of the American who was captured by cannibals and brought before the chief prior to being roasted alive. He was astonished when he heard the chieftain speak with a perfect Harvard accent.

"Did your years in Harvard do nothing to change you?" the American asked.

"Of course they did. They civilized me. After you're roasted, I shall dress for dinner and eat you with knife and fork."

145

"Your error is that you seek God outside of you," said the Master.

"Shall I then seek God inside?"

"Do you not see that your 'inside' is outside of you?" said the Master.

146

The Master constantly reminded people of their robot-like existence: "How can you call yourself human if every one of your thoughts, feelings, and actions is mechanical, arising not from yourself but from your conditioning?"

"Can anything break the conditioning and set us free?" the disciples asked.

"Yes. Awareness." Then after a moment's thought, the Master added, "And catastrophe."

"Catastrophe?"

"Yes. A very English Englishman once told me that after being shipwrecked with another Englishman for a whole hour, he finally succeeded in breaking loose from his conditioning and spoke without being introduced!"

"What did he say?"

"Pardon me for speaking to you without being introduced, but is this the way to Southampton?"

147

The Master persistently warned against the attempt to encompass Reality in a concept or in a name.

A scholar in mysticism once asked, "When you speak of 'being,' sir, is it eternal, transcendent being you speak of or transient, contingent being?"

The Master closed his eyes in thought. Then he opened them, put on his most disarming expression, and said, "Yes!"

Later the Master said, "As soon as you put a name to Reality, it ceases to be Reality."

"Even when you call it 'Reality'?" asked a mischievous disciple.

"Precisely. Even when you call it 'it.'"

148

The most common cause of unhappiness, the Master claimed, is the decision people make to be unhappy. That is why, of two people who find themselves in exactly the same situation, one is happy, the other miserable.

The Master told how his little daughter had been reluctant to go to summer camp. In an attempt to ease her misgivings, the Master addressed several postcards to himself and gave them to the child.

"Every day," he said, "just write 'I'm fine' on one of these cards and drop it in the mailbox."

The girl pondered this and asked, "How do you spell *miserable?*"

149

The Master made it his task to destroy systematically every doctrine, every belief, every concept of the divine, for these things, which were originally intended as pointers, were now being taken as descriptions.

He loved to quote the Eastern saying "When the sage points to the moon, all that the idiot sees is the finger."

150

The Master argued with no one, for he knew that what the arguer sought was confirmation of his beliefs, not the truth.

He once showed them the value of an argument:

"Does a slice of bread fall with the buttered side up or down?"

"With the buttered side down, of course."

"No, with the buttered side up."

"Let's put it to the test."

So a slice of bread was buttered and thrown up in the air. It fell buttered side up.

"I win!"

"Only because I made a mistake."

"What mistake?"

"I obviously buttered the wrong side."

151

"A religious belief," said the Master, "is not a statement of Reality but a clue about something that is a mystery, beyond the grasp of human thought. In short, a religious belief is only a finger pointing to the moon.

"Some religious people never get beyond the study of the finger. Others are engaged in sucking it. Others yet use the finger to gouge their eyes out. These are the bigots whom religion has made blind.

"Rare indeed is the religionist who is sufficiently detached from the finger to see what it is indicating. These are those who, having gone beyond belief, are taken for blasphemers."

152

One night the Master led his disciples into the open fields below a star-studded sky. Then, pointing toward the stars, he looked at the disciples and said, "Now concentrate on my finger, everyone."

They got the point.

153

Alarmed at the Master's tendency to destroy every statement of belief in God, one disciple cried out, "I'm left with nothing to hold on to!"

"That's what the fledgling says when pushed out of its nest," said the Master.

Later he said, "Do you expect to fly when you are securely settled in the nest of your beliefs? That isn't flying. That's flapping your wings!"

154

"Humility is not silly self-deprecation," said the Master. "It comes from understanding that all you succeed in doing by your efforts is changing your behavior, not yourself."

"So true change is effortless?"

"That's right," said the Master.

"And how does it come about?"

"Through awareness," said the Master.

"And what does one do to become aware?"

"What does one do, when one is asleep, to wake from sleep?" said the Master.

155

"So there is no true good that one can take pride in?" a disciple asked.

In reply, the Master told of a conversation he overheard:

"Our Master! What a voice he has! How divinely he chants!"

"Huh! If I had his voice, I'd chant just as well!"

156

Said the self-righteous preacher, "What, in your judgment, is the greatest sin in the world?"

"That of the person who sees other human beings as sinners," said the Master.

157

"There are, indeed, two types of human beings: the Pharisees and the publicans," said the Master after reading a parable of Jesus.

"How does one recognize the Pharisees?"

"Simple. They are the ones who do the classifying!" said the Master.

158

When the ruler of a neighboring kingdom announced his intention of visiting the monastery, everyone was excited. Only the Master was his usual self.

The king was ushered into the presence of the Master. He bowed low in greeting and said, "It is my belief that you have attained mystical perfection. So I have come to ask about the essence of the mystical."

"Why?" said the Master.

"It is my wish to inquire into the nature of being so as to be able to control my own being and that of my subjects and bring my nation into harmony."

"Good," said the Master. "But I must warn you that when you have gone far enough in your inquiry, you will discover that the harmony you seek is achieved not through control but through surrender."

159

"All human beings are about equally good or bad," said the Master, who hated to use those labels.

"How can you put a saint on an equal footing with a sinner?" protested a disciple.

"Because everyone is the same distance from the sun. Does it really lessen the distance if you live on top of a skyscraper?"

160

The Master maintained that what the whole world held to be true is false, so the pioneer is always in a minority of one.

He said, "You think of truth as if it were a formula that you can pick up from a book. Truth is purchased at the price of loneliness. If you wish to follow truth, you must learn to walk alone."

161

"I am ready to go anywhere in search of truth," proclaimed the ardent disciple.

The Master was amused. "When are you going to set out?" he asked.

"The moment you tell me where to go."

"I suggest you travel in the direction in which your nose is pointing."

"Yes. But where do I stop?"

"Anywhere you wish."

"And will truth be there?"

"Yes. Right in front of your nose, staring your unseeing eyes in the face."

162

"Is Enlightenment easy or difficult?"

"It is as easy and as difficult as seeing what is right before your eyes."

"How can seeing what is right before one's eyes be difficult?"

To that the Master responded with the following anecdote:

A girl greeted her boyfriend. "Notice anything different about me?"

"New dress?"

"No."

"New shoes?"

"No. Something else."

"I give up."

"I'm wearing a gas mask."

163

The disciple was a Buddhist. "What is the mind of Buddha?" he asked.

"Why not ask about your own mind or self instead of someone else's?" said the Master.

"Then what is my self, O Master?"

"For that you have to learn what is known as 'the secret act.' "

"What is the secret act?"

"This," said the Master, as he closed his eyes and opened them.

164

The Master explained to his disciples that Enlightenment would come if they achieved noninterpretative looking.

What, they wanted to know, was interpretative looking?

This is how the Master explained it:

A couple of Catholic laborers were paving the road in front of a brothel when they saw a rabbi slink into the house of ill repute.

"Well, what can you expect?" they said to each other.

After a while, a parson slipped in. No surprise. "What can you expect?"

Then came the local Catholic priest, who covered his face with a cloak just before he dove into the building. "Now isn't that dreadful? One of the women must have taken ill."

165

A disciple once asked the Master how he could enter the Path.

"Do you hear the murmur of that stream as it passes by the monastery?"

"Yes."

"That is an excellent way to enter the Path."

166

The Master loved to tell this story about himself:

After his first child was born, he went to the nursery and saw his wife standing over the baby's crib. Silently he watched her as she gazed at the sleeping infant. In her face he saw wonder, incredulity, rapture, ecstasy. Moved to tears, he tiptoed over to her, put an arm round her waist, and whispered, "I know exactly what you must feel, my dear."

Startled into consciousness, his wife blurted out, "Yes. For the life of me, I don't see how they can make a crib like that for twenty bucks."

167

Whenever the topic of God came up, the Master would insist that God is essentially beyond the grasp of human thought—a mystery—so anything said about God was true not of God but of our concept of God.

The disciples never really grasped the implications of this until the Master one day undertook to show them.

"It is not true to say that God created the world or God loves us or God is great, for of God nothing may be said. So, in the interest of accuracy, we should say, 'Our God-concept created the world. Our God-concept loves us. Our God-concept is great.' "

"If that is true, should we not drop every concept we have of the divine?"

"There would be no need to abandon your idols if you did not construct them in the first place," said the Master.

168

It bothered some of the disciples that the Master seemed to care so little whether or not people believed in a personal God.

He once quoted to them a favorite sentence from the diary of United Nations Secretary General Dag Hammarskjold:

"God does not die on the day we cease to believe in a personal deity, but we die on the day when our lives cease to be illumined by the steady radiance, renewed daily, of a *wonder*, the source of which is beyond all reason."*

* *Markings*. New York: Alfred A. Knopf, 1965.

169

The Master once saw a large crowd assembled at the monastery gate singing hymns at him and holding up a banner that read "Christ Is the Answer."

After walking over to the dour-looking man who held the sign, the Master asked, "Yes, but what is the question?"

The man was momentarily taken aback but recovered quickly enough to say, "Christ is not the answer to a question, but the answer to our problems."

"In that case, what is the problem?"

Later he said to his disciples, "If Christ is, indeed, the answer, then this is what Christ means: the clear understanding of *who* is creating the problem, and how."

170

Human problems stubbornly resist ideological solutions. The labor reformer discovered this to his dismay when he took the Master to watch a trench being dug with modern methods. "This machine," he said, "has taken jobs from scores of men. They ought to destroy it and put a hundred men with shovels in that ditch."

"Yes," said the Master. "Or better still, a thousand men with teaspoons."

171

"What can I do to attain Enlightenment?" asked the eager disciple.

"See Reality as it is," said the Master.

"Well, what can I do to see Reality as it is?"

The Master smiled and said, "I have good news and bad news for you, my friend."

"What's the bad news?"

"There's nothing you can do to see—it's a gift."

"And what's the good news?"

"There's nothing you can do to see—it's a gift."

172

The preacher was determined to extract from the Master a clear declaration of belief in God.

"Do you believe there is a God?"

"Of course I do," said the Master.

"And God made everything. Do you believe that?"

"Yes, yes," said the Master. "I certainly do."

"And who made God?"

"You," said the Master.

The preacher was aghast. "Do you seriously mean to tell me that it is I who made God?"

"The one you are forever *thinking* about and *talking* about—yes," said the Master placidly.

173

The Master dismissed ideologues for the simple reason that their theories sounded reasonable but would never fit Reality.

He told of an ideologue who said, "This is a crazy world. The rich buy on credit though they have plenty of money, but the poor, who are penniless, must pay cash."

"So what do you suggest?" someone asked.

"Turn things around. Make the rich pay cash and give the poor credit."

"But if a shopkeeper gives credit to the poor, he'll end up poor himself."

"Great!" said the ideologue. "Then he can buy on credit too!"

174

The Master found it tiresome to speak with people who were forever bent on defending the existence of God and discussing God's nature while neglecting the all-important task of self-awareness, which alone could bring them love and liberation.

To a group of people who asked him to speak to them of God, the Master said, "What you seek, alas, is to talk of God rather than see God; and you see God as you *think* God is, not as God *actually* is. For God is manifest, not hidden. Why talk? Open your eyes and see."

Later he added, "Seeing is the easiest thing in the world. All you need to do is raise the shutters of your God-thoughts."

175

Said a disciple, "We have to dress and eat. How do we get out of all that?"

"We eat. We dress," said the Master.

"I do not understand."

"If you don't understand, get dressed and eat your food."

Later the Master said, "You never rise above anything you avoid facing."

Later still, "People who want to rise above a well-cooked meal and a well-tailored garment are out of their spiritual minds."

176

The Master was a great supporter of historical research. His one complaint about history students, however, was that they generally passed over the most valuable lessons that history has to offer.

"For instance?" asked one student.

"For instance, the sight of problems, once so vital, but now no more than cold abstractions in a book. The characters in history's drama, once thought to be so mighty, but in reality mere puppets pulled by strings so obvious to us, so pathetically unsuspected by them!"

177

"What does it mean to be Enlightened?"

"To see."

"What?"

"The hollowness of success, the emptiness of achievements, the nothingness of human striving," said the Master.

The disciple was appalled. "But isn't that pessimism and despair?"

"No. That's the excitement and freedom of the eagle gliding over a bottomless ravine."

178

Said the Master, "What you call a friendship is really a business deal: Live up to my expectations, give me what I want, and I shall love you. Refuse me, and my love sours into resentment and indifference."

He told of the man who, at the end of a day, came home to his wife and his three-year-old daughter.

"Have you a kiss for Daddy?"

"No."

"I'm ashamed of you. Your daddy works hard all day to bring home a little money, and this is how you behave! Come on now, where's the kiss?"

Looking him in the eye, the cute three-year-old said, "Where's the money?"

179

Said a disciple, "I don't trade my love for money."

Said the Master, "Isn't it as bad—or worse—that you trade it for love?"

180

A despondent disciple complained that, because of his handicaps, he was being cheated by life.

"Cheated?" cried the Master. "Cheated? Look around you, man! With every moment of consciousness, you are being grossly overpaid!"

181

The Master followed that up with the story of the hotel owner who complained bitterly about the effect on his business of a new highway the government had built.

"Look," said a friend. "I just don't understand you. I see a no vacancy sign each night in front of your hotel."

"You can't go by that. Before they built the highway, I used to turn away thirty or forty people each day. Now I never turn away more than twenty-five."

Added the Master, "When you are determined to feel bad, even nonexistent customers are real."

182

That reminded the disciples of the pessimist who said, "Life is so awful; it would have been better not to have been born."

"Yes," replied the Master, with a twinkle in his eye. "But how many have that kind of luck? One in ten thousand, maybe."

183

The Master must have known that his words were frequently beyond his disciples' comprehension. He spoke to them nonetheless, in the knowledge that a day would surely come when his words would take root and blossom in the hearts of those who heard them.

One day he said, "Time always seems so long when you wait—for a vacation, an examination, for something yearned for or dreaded in the future.

"But to those who dare to surrender to the experience of the present moment—with no thought about the experience, no desire that it return or be avoided—time is transformed into the radiance of eternity."

184

"You are destroyed by life's tranquility," said the Master to an easygoing disciple. "Only disaster can save you."

And this is how he explained it:

"Throw a frog into a pan of boiling water, and it will jump out in a second. Place it in a pan of water that is heated very gradually, and it will lose the tension to spring when the moment to leap arrives."

185

Said the governor, "Is there any advice you can give me in the exercise of my office?"

"Yes. Learn how to give orders."

"Why?"

"So that others can receive them without feeling inferior," said the Master.

186

When asked how one discovered silence, the Master told this story:

A factory was interested in buying bullfrog skins. A farmer wired the company that he could supply any quantity up to a hundred thousand on demand. The company wired back: "Send first consignment, fifty thousand."

Two weeks later, a single pathetic frog skin came through the mail with this note: "Sirs, I apologize. This is all the frog skins there were in the neighborhood. The noise certainly fooled me."

187

Later the Master said, "Investigate the noise that people make. Then see through the noise that you yourself are making, and you will find nothing, emptiness—and silence."

188

"My life is like shattered glass," said the visitor. "My soul is tainted with evil. Is there any hope for me?"

"Yes," said the Master. "There is something whereby each broken thing is bound again and every stain made clean."

"What?"

"Forgiveness."

"Whom do I forgive?"

"Everyone. Life, God, your neighbor. And especially yourself."

"How is that done?"

"By understanding that no one is to blame," said the Master. *"No one."*

189

It scandalized people to hear the Master say that true religion was not a social matter. He told them this parable:

There was a little polar bear who asked his mother, "Mommy, was my daddy also a polar bear?"

"Of course he was a polar bear."

After a while, "Tell me, Mommy, was my grandfather also a polar bear?"

"Yes, he was also a polar bear."

"What about my great-grandfather? Was he a polar bear too?"

"Yes, he was. Why are you asking?"

"Because I'm freezing."

The Master concluded, "Religion is neither social nor inherited. It is an intensely personal thing."

190

"I seek the meaning of existence," said the stranger.

"You are, of course, assuming," said the Master, "that existence has a meaning."

"Doesn't it?"

"When you experience existence as it is—not as you *think* it is—you will discover that your question has no meaning," said the Master.

191

"Isn't there such a thing as social liberation?"

"Of course there is," said the Master.

"How would you describe it?"

"Liberation from the need to belong to the herd," said the Master.

192

"My friend," said the Master to the freedom fighter in prison, "you will face your execution valiantly tomorrow. Only one thing holds you back from meeting death with joy."

"What is it?"

"The wish that your exploits be remembered."

"Is there anything wrong with that?" asked the condemned man.

"Has it ever struck you that if posterity remembers, it is not *you* that your actions will be attached to, but your *name*?"

"Aren't the two things the same?"

"Ah no, my friend! Your name is the sound you respond to. Your label. Who are *you*?"

That was all the man needed to die that very night—even before the firing squad came for him at dawn.

193

Word of the Master's conversation with the executed man leaked out to the disciples.

"Surely one's name is something more than a sound," they said.

In response, the Master told them about the street vendor who became a millionaire. Instead of his signature on a check, he would mark checks with two crosses because he was illiterate.

One day the banker was surprised to see three crosses on a check. "It's my wife," said the millionaire by way of explanation. "She has social ambitions. The second X in the row is my middle name."

194

The disciples were sitting on the bank of a river.

"If I fall off this bank, will I drown?" one of them asked.

"No," said the Master. "It isn't falling in that causes you to drown, it's staying in."

195

When commenting on Jesus' image of people who strained at gnats and swallowed camels, the Master explained how once, during the war, he herded everyone into the monastery basement during a vicious air raid.

All day they sat there while bombs fell around them. When evening came, two of the men could take it no longer. "We've had enough," they said. "Bombs or no bombs, we're going home."

They walked away but were back in the basement three minutes later.

"I see you've changed your minds," said the Master with a smile.

"Yes," they said, annoyed. "It's started to rain."

196

"How joyful the Master seems," a visitor remarked.

Said a disciple, "One always treads with a joyful step when one has dropped the burden called the ego."

197

The Master was asked what he thought of the achievements of modern technology. This was his reply:

An absentminded professor was late for his lecture. He jumped into a cab and shouted, "Hurry! At top speed!"

As the cab sped along, the professor realized he hadn't told the driver where to go. So he shouted, "Do you know where I want to go?"

"No, sir," said the cabbie, "but I'm driving as fast as I can."

198

A large crowd of friends and former disciples gathered to celebrate the Master's ninetieth birthday.

Before the party was over, the Master rose to speak. "Life," he said, "is measured by the quality, not by the number, of one's days."

199

When a mammoth meeting was called to protest against the government's manufacture of nuclear bombs, the Master and his disciples were conspicuous in the crowd.

Loud applause greeted the statement "Bombs kill people!"

The Master shook his head and muttered, "That isn't true. *People* kill people!"

When he realized he had been overheard by the man standing next to him, he leaned over and said, "Well, I'll correct that. *Ideas* kill people."

200

The Master made sure the monastery library was well stocked with books on every conceivable subject—politics, architecture, philosophy, poetry, agriculture, history, science, psychology, art, and the section he himself used the most, fiction.

He repeated one refrain: "God save us from people who do not *think, think, think*!"

There was nothing he feared more, he said, than the one-track mind, the one-book fanatic.

This puzzled the disciples, for it was so out of tune with the nonthinking perception, the nonconceptual awareness that was the mainstay of the Master's teaching.

When asked directly, he ambiguously replied, "A thorn can be dislodged by means of another thorn, can't it?"

201

The Master had a large skull-and-bones caution sign set up in the monastery library. It read "Books Kill."

"Why?" someone wanted to know.

"Because books breed ideas that can freeze into beliefs, thereby causing a hardening of the mind and a distorted perception of Reality."

202

A disciple complained about the Master's habit of knocking down all the disciple's beliefs.

Said the Master, "I set fire to the temple of your beliefs, for when it is destroyed you will have an unimpeded view of the vast, unbounded sky."

203

The Master met a very old neighbor who was shuffling along with a cane in his hand.

"Good morning," the Master called out. "And how are you these days?"

"Not well," said the man in a feeble voice. "I used to walk around the block every morning before breakfast. Now I feel so weak I can only get halfway and then have to turn around and come back."

204

The Master never seemed to have his fill of gazing at his firstborn child.

"What do you want him to be when he grows up?" someone asked.

"Outrageously happy," said the Master.

205

The Master stressed awareness over worship.

"But mustn't we depend on God?" he was asked.

Said the Master, "The lover desires the good of the beloved, which requires, among other things, the liberation of the beloved from the lover."

206

Later the Master enacted an imaginary dialogue between God and a devotee:

Devotee: Please don't leave me, God.

God: I go so that the holy spirit may come.

Devotee: What's this holy spirit?

God: The fearlessness and freedom that comes from nondependence.

207

The Master once told of a neighbor in the countryside who had an obsession with acquiring land.

"I wish I had more land," he said one day.

"But why?" asked the Master. "Don't you have enough already?"

"If I had more land, I could raise more cows."

"And what would you do with them?"

"Sell them and make money."

"For what?"

"To buy more land and raise a lot of cows."

208

The preacher took issue with the Master on the matter of dependence on God.

"God is our father," he said, "and we never cease to need God's help."

Said the Master, "When a father helps his infant child, all the world smiles. When a father helps his grown-up child, all the world weeps!"

209

The Master had very definite views on family planning. For all those who contended that the size of a family was the private concern of parents or the internal affair of a country, he had the following parable:

There was once a country where it became possible for citizens to develop and acquire their own nuclear bombs. They were small bombs, the size of hand grenades, but powerful enough to blow up an entire city.

A bitter debate raged over the right of private citizens to possess such explosives till they came to the following compromise: No one would be allowed to carry a nuclear bomb in public without a license. But what people did in their homes was their own private concern.

210

Someone told the Master of the phenomenal increase in the circulation of a sex magazine.

"Too bad," was his comment. "Of sex, as of Reality, it may be said that the more you read about it, the less you know it."

Later he added, "And the less you enjoy it."

211

"The modern world is suffering increasingly from sexual anorexia," said the psychiatrist.

"What's that?" said the Master.

"A loss of appetite for sex."

"How terrible!" said the Master. "What's the cure for it?"

"We don't know. Do you?"

"I think I do."

"What?"

"Make sex a sin again," said the Master with an impish smile.

212

Jesus set up the birds of the air and the flowers of the field as models for humans to imitate. So did the Master. He often told of the letter he received from an affluent neighbor:

Dear Sir,

This concerns the birdbath I donated to the monastery garden. I'm writing to inform you that it is not to be used by the sparrows.

213

While the Master did not oppose the practice of psychotherapy and even claimed that it was necessary for some people, he made no secret of his opinion that a psychotherapist merely brings relief. The psychotherapist does not really solve your problem, the Master said, he simply exchanges it for another, more comfortable one.

The Master recalled sitting in a bus after the war, intrigued by a passenger holding a heavy object wrapped in newspaper.

"What's that you've got on your lap?" the bus conductor demanded.

"An unexploded bomb. I'm taking it to the fire department."

"Heavens above, man! You don't want to carry a thing like that on your lap! Put it under your seat!"

214

The Master had this story to tell about the way people look at other people:

Soon after his marriage, the Master lived for a while on the tenth floor of a city apartment. His young wife one day stepped out of the shower to reach for a towel. She froze. There, outside the window, was a window washer looking at her. A whole minute passed as she stood rooted to the ground, too stunned to move a muscle.

The man broke the spell. "What's the matter, lady?" he said. "Haven't you ever seen a window washer?"

215

"Congratulate me!"

"Why?"

"At last I've found a job that offers excellent prospects for advancement."

Said the Master somberly, "You were a sleepwalker yesterday. You are sleepwalking today. You will sleepwalk till the day you die. What sort of advancement is that?"

"I was talking about financial advancement, not spiritual advancement."

"Ah! I see. A sleepwalker with a bank account that he isn't awake to enjoy!"

216

"Enlightenment," said the Master when asked about it, "is an awakening. Right now you are asleep and do not know it."

Then he went on to tell them of the recently married woman who complained about her husband's drinking habits.

"If you knew he drank, why did you marry him?" she was asked.

"I had no idea he drank," said the woman, "till one night he came home sober!"

217

"Allow me to explain the good news my religion proclaims," said the preacher.

The Master was all attention.

"God is love. And God loves and rewards us forever if we observe God's commandments."

"*If*?" said the Master. "Then the news isn't all that good, is it?"

218

A badly wrapped parcel of Bibles arrived at the post office and burst open, scattering beautiful calf-bound, gilt-edged books all over the floor.

A postman could not resist the temptation to help himself to one.

When the postman confessed this later, the Master said, "But what on earth made you steal a Bible?"

"My religious disposition," said the man contritely.

219

"Some people claim there is no life after death," said a disciple.

"Do they?" said the Master noncommittally.

"Wouldn't it be awful to die and never again see or hear or love or move?"

"You find that awful?" said the Master. "But that's how most people are even before they die."

220

The Master would sometimes regale visitors with tales of the redoubtable Mullah Nasruddin.

Nasruddin was once tossing about in bed. Said his wife, "What's the matter? Go to sleep!"

The mullah confessed he did not have the seven silver coins he owed his neighbor Abdullah and had to pay the following day. So he was too worried to be able to sleep.

His wife promptly got up, threw a shawl around her shoulders, went across the street, and shouted, "Abdullah! Abdullah!" till old Abdullah came to the window, asking, "What is it? What's the matter?"

The woman called out, "I just want you to know you are not going to get your silver coins tomorrow. My husband doesn't have them."

With that she walked back home and said, "Go to sleep, Nasruddin. Now Abdullah can worry."

The Master concluded, "Someone has to pay. Does anyone have to worry?"

221

To protect their crops, the farmers had killed countless numbers of birds. As he saw their corpses strewn all over the place, a disciple recalled the saying of Jesus: "Not one of these birds falls to the ground without your Father's consent." He asked the Master if that sentence made any sense.

"Yes, it does," said the Master. "But those words reveal their inner beauty only if seen against the background of these birds that breed by the million and are then slaughtered as pests."

222

"What, concretely, is Enlightenment?"

"Seeing Reality as it is," said the Master.

"Doesn't everyone see Reality as it is?"

"Oh, no! Most people see it as they think it is."

"What's the difference?"

"The difference between thinking you are drowning in a stormy sea and knowing you cannot drown because there isn't any water in sight for miles around."

223

A psychiatrist came to see the Master. "How do you deal with neurotics?" he asked.

Said the Master, "I liberate them."

"But how?"

"Rather than solve their problem, I dissolve the ego that caused it."

"How could I myself do that?"

"Get out of the prison of your thoughts and into the world of the senses," said the Master.

224

When the preacher returned to the good news theme, the Master interrupted him.

"What sort of good news is it," he asked, "that makes it so easy to go to hell and so hard to get to heaven?"

225

To illustrate the fact that there simply aren't any satisfactory symbols for God, the Master told of the time his wife was driving him through a crowded city street.

She collided with an approaching car. The driver rolled his window down and yelled, "Lady, why didn't you signal what you wanted to do?"

"Because," she answered defiantly, "there is no signal for what I wanted to do."

226

One day the Master looked at the preacher sitting there in front of him, smug in his beliefs, self-righteous in his good deeds, and he said, "My friend, I sometimes feel that when you come to die, you will die without ever having lived. It will be as if life has passed you by."

Then, as an afterthought, he added, "No, it's worse than that. Life and you have gone in opposite directions."

227

The Master was certainly no stranger to what goes on in the world.

When he was asked to explain one of his favorite sayings—"There is no good or ill but thinking makes it so"—the Master said, "Have you ever observed that what people call congestion in a train becomes atmosphere in a nightclub?"

228

To illustrate the same axiom, he one day told how, as a child, he overheard his father, a famous politician, sharply criticize a party member who had crossed over to the opposition.

"But, Father, the other day you were all praise for the man who left the opposition to join your party."

"Well, my son, you might as well learn this important truth early in life: Those who go over to the other party are traitors. Those who come to ours are converts."

229

"In the land of Enlightenment, your learning is of as little use as clubs are in modern warfare. What is needed here is awareness," said the Master.

And he followed that statement up with the story of a disciple who hired a Latvian refugee as a housemaid, then found to her dismay that the young woman couldn't run a vacuum cleaner, operate a mixer, or cope with a washing machine.

"What *can* you do?" the disciple asked.

The young woman smiled in quiet pride. "I can milk a reindeer."

230

"How long will it take me to solve my problem?"

"Not one minute more than it takes you to understand it," said the Master.

231

The preacher was an unusual man. People trembled when they saw him. He never laughed and was tenacious in his ascetical practices, for he believed in self-inflicted pain. He was known to fast frequently and to wear inadequate clothing in the winter.

One day he told the Master of a secret pain. "I have lived a life of abnegation and been faithful to the precepts of my religion. But there's something that eludes me, and I cannot find out what. Can you?"

The Master looked at him, so hard and dry, and said, "Yes. Soul."

232

The Master told this tale to show how cleverness is an obstacle to Enlightenment:

There were three passengers in a plane—Big Brain, a Boy Scout, and a bishop. The plane developed engine trouble, and the pilot announced he was bailing out. There were only three parachutes, and he was taking one. The others would have to decide which of them were going to be saved. Big Brain said, "Because I am necessary to the country, I should have a parachute." So he grabbed one and jumped.

The bishop looked at the Boy Scout. "Son, I have lived a long life, so I think it fitting that you should have the remaining parachute. I am ready to die."

"That won't be necessary, Bishop," said the Boy Scout. "There are two parachutes here. Big Brain just jumped out with my knapsack."

Added the Master, "Cleverness ordinarily leaves no room for awareness."

233

Visitors were always struck by the Master's leisurely manner.

"I just don't have the time to be in a hurry," he would say.

234

To a group of social activists who sought his blessing on a plan they were about to put into action, the Master said, "What you need, I'm afraid, is light, not action."

Later he explained, "To fight evil with activity is like fighting darkness with one's hands. So what you need is light, not fight."

235

It was quite impossible to get the Master to take the idea of patriotism or nationalism seriously.

He once told of an Englishman who was upbraided by a relative for becoming an American citizen. "What have you gained by becoming an American?" his relative asked.

"Well," the Englishman explained, "for one thing, I win the American Revolution."

236

The Master once gave an address on the danger of religion, affirming, among other things, that religious people all too easily use God to cover up their pettiness and self-seeking.

This provoked a sharp rejoinder in the form of a book wherein as many as a hundred religious leaders wrote articles to refute the Master's words.

The Master smiled when he saw the book. "If what I said was wrong, one article would have been enough," he said.

237

After delivering a stirring political speech at a rally, a disciple asked the Master what he thought of it.

Said the Master, "If what you said was true, where was the need to shout?"

And later, he said to all the disciples, "Truth suffers more from the heat of its defenders than from all the attacks of its opponents."

238

The Master once exposed his disciples by means of the following lesson:

He gave each of them a sheet of paper and asked them to write down the length of the hall they were in.

Almost everyone gave flat figures like fifty feet. Two or three added the word *approximately*.

Said the Master, "No one gave the right answer."

"What is the right answer?" they asked.

"The right answer is 'I do not know.' "

239

The Master deplored the evils of competition.

"Doesn't competition bring out the best in us?" he was asked.

"It brings out the worst in you, because it teaches you to hate."

"Hate what?"

"Yourself, for you allow your activity to be determined by your competitor, not by your own needs and limitations. Others, for you seek to get ahead at their expense."

"But that would sound the death knell of change and progress," someone protested.

Said the Master, "The only progress there is, is love-progress. The only change worth having is a change of heart."

240

"Why do so many people not attain Enlightenment?" someone asked the Master.

"Because they see as loss what is actually a gain."

Then he told of an acquaintance who went into business. Trade flourished. There was a constant run of customers.

When the Master congratulated him on how well he was doing, the man said mournfully, "Let's take a realistic view of things, sir. Look at those front doors. If so many people continue to push through them, we'll soon have to replace the hinges."

241

To a merchant who escaped from the pain of life into money-making, the Master said, "There was once a man who feared his own footprints. So, instead of walking, he took to running, which only increased the number of footprints he made. What he needed to do was stop."

242

"My suffering is unbearable."

Said the Master, "The present moment is never unbearable. It is what you think is coming in the next five minutes or the next five days that drives you to despair. Stop living in the future."

243

Hearing someone announce himself a doctor of theology, the Master, who was quite a tease, said with an innocent air, "A doctor of *theology*? What kind of disease is that?"

244

It was well known that the Master had little use for *theology*, as the word is commonly understood.

When asked point-blank about it, the Master said, "Theology has become an evil because it is not so much a quest for truth, as the maintenance of a belief system."

245

The Master held that the loyalty of theologians to their belief systems made them all too prone to turn a blind eye to the truth and to reject the Messiah when he appeared.

Philosophers fared better at his hands. Being unfettered by beliefs, they were more open in their quest, he said.

But even philosophy, alas, was limited, for it relied on words and concepts to penetrate a Reality that was susceptible only to the nonconceptualizing mind.

"Philosophy," he once remarked, "is a disease that is cured only by Enlightenment. Then it gives way to parables and silence."

246

When asked what kind of funeral he wanted for himself, the Master said, "Leave my body in a desert place and do not bother to dig a grave, so earth and sky will be my coffin, the moon and stars my funeral lamps, and all creation the funeral flowers."

"We'd rather cremate your body," said the disciples.

"That would be too much trouble," said the Master. "And why deprive the kites and ants of a funeral banquet?"

247

"Why is it so hard for a rich man to enter the kingdom of God?"

In reply, the Master told of a man who arrived at a hotel in his limousine and was carried to his room on a stretcher. The manager, thinking the man was paralyzed, asked his wife what the matter was. The woman replied, "He's a very rich man. He doesn't need to walk."

248

The disciples told the Master of the epitaph they had designed for him:

It Was Easier
To Be Fearless
When He Was Around.

Said the Master, "If in order to be fearless you needed me, my presence only served to conceal your cowardice, not to cure it."

249

The governor announced that he was coming to see a monastery bush that was full of exotic roses.

When he got to the monastery garden, he found there was only one rose on the bush. When he learned that the Master had cut all the other roses, he demanded to know why.

"Because," said the Master, "had I left all the roses on the bush, you would not have seen even one of them."

Then, after a pause, he added, "You have grown accustomed to multitudes, my friend. When did you last see a person?"

250

"What must I do to attain the divine?"

"The divine isn't something one attains through doing, but something one realizes through seeing," said the Master.

"What, then, is the function of doing?"

"To express the divine, not to attain it."

251

This is how the Master illustrated the attitude of affluent nations today:

A man is awakened from sleep by the nudgings of his wife. "Get up and close the window. It is freezing outside."

The man sighs. "For heaven's sake! If I close the window, will that make it warm outside?"

252

The Master would allow his disciples to live with him only for a limited period of time; then he would push them away to fend for themselves.

A newcomer questioning a disciple about this practice of the Master received this reply: "The Master is a mirror that reflects Reality and you. Once you have seen Reality, the mirror must be flung away lest, through your veneration, it turn into a screen."

253

"How can I change myself?"

"You are yourself, so you can no more change *yourself* than you can walk away from your feet."

"Is there nothing I can do then?"

"You can understand and accept this."

"How will I change if I accept myself?"

"How will you change if you don't? What you don't accept, you do not change, you merely manage to repress."

254

"Why do I do evil?"

"Because you are bewitched," said the Master.

"By what?"

"The illusory thing you call *self*."

"So how will evil cease?"

"Through understanding that the self as you know it does not exist, so it need not be protected."

255

To a woman who rhapsodized about the beauties of love, the Master told the story of Nasruddin, who was attempting to console his dying wife in every possible way.

His wife opened her eyes and said, "It is certain that this night will be my last. I shall not see the sun again. Nasruddin, how will you take my death?"

"How will I take your death? I will go mad."

Serious as her condition was, his wife could not repress a smile. "Ah, you cunning fellow," she said. "I know you. You won't stay unmarried for even a month after my death."

"What do you mean?" asked Nasruddin indignantly. "Of course I will go mad—but I won't go that mad."

256

"What is the cause of evil?"

"Ignorance," said the Master.

"And how is it dispelled?"

"Not by effort, but by light. By understanding, not by action."

Later the Master added, "The sign of Enlightenment is peace. You stop fleeing when you see you are being pursued only by the fantasies your fears have fabricated."

257

The Master had no illusions about what people ordinarily call love. He recalled a conversation he'd overheard between a politician and his friend:

"Did you know that our association's vice president is planning to run against you in the coming elections?"

"That scoundrel! I'm not one bit afraid. Everyone knows that man wasn't in jail only because of his political connections."

"Our secretary is planning to announce his candidacy too."

"What! Doesn't he fear exposure for embezzlement?"

"Well now! I was only joking. Actually I've just met both of them, and they're both supporting your campaign."

"Now see what you've done! You've made me say nasty things about two of the nicest men in our association."

258

"Why do you never preach repentance?" asked the preacher.

"It's the only thing I teach," said the Master.

"But I never hear you speak on sorrow for sin."

"Repentance isn't sorrow for the past. The past is dead and isn't worth a moment's grief. Repentance is a change of mind, a radically different vision of Reality."

259

The philosopher gave the Master a lengthy disquisition of "objective reality."

Said the Master, "What you know is not Reality, but your perception of it. What you experience is not the world, but your own state of mind."

"Can Reality ever be grasped then?"

"Yes, but only by those who go beyond their thoughts."

"What sort of people are these?"

"Those who have lost the great projector called the self; for when self is lost, projection stops and the world is seen in its naked loveliness."

260

When the Master heard someone say, "I'd like my wife a lot better if she were a different kind of woman," the Master recalled the time he was admiring a sunset at sea.

"Isn't it lovely?" he exclaimed to a woman standing at the rail nearby.

"Yes," said the woman reluctantly. "But don't you think there should be a little more pink on the left side?"

Said the Master, "Everyone looks lovely when you shed your jaundiced expectations of what she should look like."

261

"I pride myself on being a good judge of character."

"Is that really something to be proud of?" asked the Master.

"Isn't it?"

"No. There's one defect a good judge has in common with a bad judge: he judges."

262

"What depresses me is the utter ordinariness of my existence. I haven't done a single important thing in my life that the world would care to notice."

"You are wrong to think that the attention of the world is what gives importance to an action," said the Master.

A lengthy pause ensued.

"Well, I haven't done a single thing to influence anyone for good or ill."

"You are wrong to think that influencing others is what gives importance to an action," said the Master.

"Well, then, what is it that gives importance to an action?"

"Doing it for its own sake with the whole of one's being. Then it becomes a nonprofit, godlike activity."

263

When one of his disciples was guilty of a serious lapse, everyone expected the Master to give him some exemplary punishment.

When nothing was done for a whole month, someone pleaded with the Master. "We cannot ignore what has happened. After all, God has given us eyes."

"Yes," replied the Master, "and eyelids!"

264

"In your sermons, why do you overemphasize the value of suffering?" said the Master.

"Because it seasons us to face whatever life may bring," the preacher replied.

The Master said nothing to that.

Later a disciple asked, "Exactly what does suffering season us to face?"

"More suffering, presumably," said the Master with a smile.

265

"Doesn't suffering season a person?"

"It's not the suffering that matters, but a person's disposition, for suffering can sweeten or embitter just as the potter's fire can char the clay or season it."

266

When asked why he never argued with anyone, the Master told of the old blacksmith who confided in a friend that his blacksmith father had wanted him to follow his profession. But his mother had set her heart on his becoming a dentist. "And you know, I'm glad my father had his way, because if I had become a dentist, I would have starved to death. And I can prove it."

"How?" asked the friend.

"Well, I've been in this smithy for thirty years, and not once in all that time has anyone asked me to pull out a tooth."

"That," the Master concluded, "is the logic that arguments are made of. When you see, you need no logic."

267

"Why are you always at your prayers?" asked the Master.

"Because prayer takes a great load off my mind."

"Unfortunately, that is what it is wont to do."

"What's so unfortunate about it?"

"It distracts you from seeing who put the load there in the first place," said the Master.

268

It amused the Master to hear the exaggerated claims of modern science to change the universe.

"In a conflict between human will and nature, back nature," he used to say.

"But can't we change anything in the universe?"

"Not until we have learned to submit to it."

269

"You listen," said the Master, "not to discover, but to find something that confirms your own thoughts. You argue, not to find the truth, but to vindicate your thinking."

And he told of a king who, passing through a small town, saw indications of amazing marksmanship everywhere. Trees and barns and fences had circles painted on them with a bullet hole in the exact center. He asked to see this unusual marksman. It turned out to be a ten-year-old child.

"This is incredible," said the king in wonder. "How in the world do you do it?"

"Easy as pie," was the answer. "I shoot first and draw the circles later."

"So you get your conclusions first and build your premises around them later," said the Master. "Isn't that the way you manage to hold on to your religion and to your ideology?"

270

Every time the preacher mentioned God, the Master would say, "Keep God out of this."

Finally the preacher could take it no longer. "I've always suspected you of being an atheist," he yelled. "Why must I keep God out of this?"

The Master gently told the following story:

A priest went to console a grieving widow. "Look what your God has done," screamed the woman.

"Death does not please God, my dear," replied the clergyman. "God deplores it just as much as you."

"Then why does God allow it?" she said angrily.

"There is no way we can know, for God is mystery."

"Then how can you know that death doesn't please God?" she yelled.

"Well, we can assume . . ."

"Shut up!" screamed the widow. "Keep God out of this, will you?"

271

The activists were aggrieved that the Master thought they needed less action and more light.

"Light on what?" they wanted to know.

"On what life is all about," said the Master.

"We certainly know that life is to be lived for others," said the activists. "What more light do we need than that?"

"You need to understand what the preposition *for* means."

272

The Master had a parable for the preacher:

A centipede went to a wise old owl and complained of the gout. Each of its hundred legs ached. What could it do? After giving the matter serious thought, the owl advised the centipede to become a squirrel. With only four legs, it would have 96 percent of its pain removed.

Said the centipede, "A splendid idea. Now tell me how I could go about becoming a squirrel."

"Don't bother me with that," said the owl. "I only create policy around here."

273

"I long to find some solid ground, some firm foundation for my life."

"Look at it like this," said the Master. "What is the solid ground of the bird migrating across continents? What is the firm foundation of the fish carried by the river to the sea?"

274

An activist returned to find out what kind of light he was still in need of.

"The light to know the difference between a lover and an activist," the Master said. "A lover participates in a symphony."

"And the activist?"

"Is caught up with the sound of his own drum."

275

The Master never tired of reminding those who swore by their Scriptures that truth cannot be grasped or expressed by the conceptualizing mind.

He told of an executive who complained to his secretary about a telephone message. "I can't read this," he said.

"I couldn't understand the caller very well," said the secretary. "So I didn't write it very clearly."

276

"Is there really nothing we can do to achieve Enlightenment?"

"Well," said the Master good-humoredly, "you could imitate the old woman who pressed against the wall of the carriage to speed the train along."

277

The preacher hotly contested the Master's teaching that there is nothing that can be done to be Enlightened.

Said the Master, "But it is you, is it not, who preach that everything is a gift from God, that all our goodness is God's grace?"

"Yes, but I also preach that God demands our cooperation."

"Ah! Like the man who chopped wood and demanded that his little son cooperate by doing the grunting," said the Master happily.

278

What newcomers found hard to adjust to was the humanity, the sheer ordinariness, of the Master. He enjoyed the good things of life and the pleasures of the senses too much to fit into their categories of what a holy man should be.

A newcomer took this up with a disciple and heard this reply: "When God makes a master, he does not unmake the man."

279

A religious-minded disciple returned to the matter of Scripture. "Do you mean to say the Scriptures can give us no notion of God at all?"

"Any God that is contained in a notion is no God at all. That is why God is a mystery—something you have no notion of," said the Master.

"Then what does Scripture offer us?"

In reply, the Master told of dining in a Chinese restaurant when one of the musicians began to play a vaguely familiar melody. No one in the group could name the tune.

The Master summoned a smartly clad waiter and asked him to find out what the man was playing. He padded across the floor, then returned to announce with pleasure, "Violin!"

280

"As your perception is, so will your action be. The thing to change is not your action but your outlook," said the Master.

"What must I do to change it?"

"Merely understand that your present way of looking is defective."

281

To illustrate his oft-repeated axiom, "You see things as you are, not as they are," the Master would tell of an eighty-one-year-old friend who came to the monastery all wet and muddy.

"It's that creek a mile away from here," he said. "I used to be able to jump right across in the old days. But nowadays I always land in the middle. I just hadn't noticed that the creek has been getting wider."

To which the Master himself added, "Nowadays I realize, each time I bend, that the ground is farther away than it used to be when I was young."

282

"There is one thing that even God cannot do," said the Master to a disciple who feared to give offense.

"What?"

"He cannot please everyone," said the Master.

283

"What you need is awareness," said the Master to the religious-minded disciple. "Awareness, awareness, awareness."

"I know. So I seek to be aware of God's presence."

"God-awareness is a fantasy, for you have no notion of what God is like. Self-awareness is what you need."

284

Later the Master said, "If God is love, then the distance between God and you is the exact distance between you and the awareness of yourself."

285

When someone insisted that there could be only one *absolutely* right answer to any given moral question, the Master said, "When people sleep in a damp place, they get lumbago. But that's not true of fish. Living on a tree can be perilous and trying on the nerves. But that's not true of monkeys.

"So of fish and monkeys and human beings, whose habitat is the right one—absolutely?

"Human beings eat flesh, buffaloes eat grass, and trees feed on the earth. Of these three, whose taste is the right one—absolutely?"

286

A young man eagerly described what he dreamed of doing for the poor.

Said the Master, "When do you propose to make your dream come true?"

"As soon as the opportunity arrives."

"Opportunity never arrives," said the Master. "It's already here."

287

An affluent man once told the Master that, try as he might, he simply couldn't stop the compulsion to make money.

"Even at the cost of enjoying life, alas," said the Master.

"I shall leave the enjoyment of life for my old age."

"If you ever live to have one," said the Master as he recounted the story of the highwayman who said, "Your money or your life!"

Said the victim, "Take my life. I'm saving my money for my old age."

288

For another wealthy man who endangered his health in his zeal for making money, the Master told the story of the miser who was being taken to his grave.

Suddenly he came to consciousness, sized up the situation, and made a quick decision: "I'd better stay put or else I'll have to pay the funeral bill."

"Most people would rather save their money than their lives," the Master concluded.

289

The disciples never quite resigned themselves to the Master's teaching that one had to "do" nothing to change or be Enlightened.

"What can you *do* to dispel darkness?" he would say. "Darkness is the absence of light. Evil, the absence of awareness. What does one *do* to an absence?"

290

"My parents told me to beware of you," said a newcomer.

The Master smiled. "Beware, my dear. Be very, very careful, and you will meet the fate of your cautious parents—nothing very good or bad will ever happen to you."

291

"I don't know if I can trust this man," said a newcomer.

Said an experienced disciple, "The Master wouldn't have us trust a single word he says. He urges us to doubt, to question, to challenge everything."

292

Later the disciple added, "It isn't the Master's words I fear. It's his presence. His words bring light, but his presence burns you up."

293

When someone expressed her hatred for the oppressors of her country, the Master replied, "Never allow anyone to drag you down so low as to make you hate him."

294

"If you search for God, you search for ideas—and miss the Reality," said the Master.

He then told of the monk who complained about the cell he had been given. "I wanted a cell from where I could contemplate the stars. In the one I have, a stupid tree blocks out the view."

It was while gazing at that particular tree that Enlightenment had come to the previous occupant of the cell.

295

"What does your master teach?"

"Nothing."

"Then what on earth does he offer?"

"As much as you wish to take of his silence and of his love and of the rays of the myriad suns that shine in the skies within him and through every leaf and blade of grass."

296

"Everyone knows I am fearless," said the governor, "but I confess to the fear of one thing: death. What is death?"

"How should I know?"

"But you are an Enlightened master!"

"Maybe. But not a dead one, yet."

297

A scientist showed the Master a documentary film on the achievements of modern science.

"Today we are able to irrigate a desert," he exulted, "harness the power of Niagara Falls, detect the composition of a distant star and the makeup of an atom. Our conquest of nature will soon be complete."

The Master was impressed but pensive.

Later he said, "Why conquer nature? Nature is our friend. Why not spend all that energy in overcoming the one single enemy of the human race: fear?"

298

When some of his disciples spoke in praise of a well-known religious leader, the Master held his peace.

When asked about this later, he said, "The man wields power over others. He is no religious leader."

"What, then, is a religious leader's function?"

"To inspire, not to legislate," said the Master. "To awaken, not coerce."

299

It baffled the disciples to hear the Master say that evil, when viewed from a higher perspective, is good, that sin is a doorway to grace.

So he told them the story of Carthage, a thorn in the flesh of ancient Rome. When Rome finally razed Carthage, she found rest, grew flabby, and decayed.

"If all evil were to disappear," concluded the Master, "the human spirit would rot."

300

"What sort of penance shall I do, given the enormity of my crimes?"

"Understand the ignorance that caused them," said the Master.

Later he added, "It is thus you will understand and forgive both others and yourself and stop calling for the revenge you refer to as punishment or penance."

301

The Master claimed that a major reason for unhappiness in the world is the secret pleasure people take in being miserable.

He told of a friend who said to his wife, "Why don't you get away and have a good time, darling?"

"Now, dear, you know perfectly well that I never enjoy a good time!"

302

A business executive asked what the Master thought was the secret of successful living.

"Make one person happy each day."

As an afterthought the Master added, "Even if that person is yourself."

A minute passed and he said, "Especially if that person is yourself."

303

When the governor came on a visit, the Master took the occasion to protest against the censorship he had imposed on the press.

Said the governor sharply, "You have no idea how dangerous the press has become lately."

Said the Master, "Only the suppressed word is dangerous."

304

Once, in the course of a talk he gave, the Master quoted from an ancient poet.

A young woman came up later to say she would rather he had quoted from the Scriptures.

"Did that pagan author whom you quoted really know God?" she said.

"Young woman," said the Master severely, "if you think that God is the author of the book you call the Scriptures, I would have you know God is also the author of a much earlier work called creation."

305

"In spirituality it isn't effort that counts," said the Master, "but surrender.

"When you fall into the water and don't know how to swim, you become frightened and say, 'I must not drown, I must not drown,' and begin to thrash about with arms and legs and, in your anxiety, swallow more water and eventually drown. Whereas if you would let go of your thoughts and efforts and allow yourself to go down to the bottom, your body would come back to the surface on its own. That's spirituality!"

306

"Sincerity is not enough," the Master would frequently say. "What you need is honesty."

"What's the difference?" someone asked.

"Honesty is a never-ending openness to the facts," said the Master. "Sincerity is believing one's own propaganda."

307

Asked about the providence of God, the Master told the story of two Jews who had fallen upon hard times.

"I know that God will provide," said one with great conviction.

"I only wish God would provide *until* he provides," said the other.

308

One day the Master said, "You are not ready to 'fight' evil until you are able to see the good it does."

This left the disciples in considerable confusion, which the Master made no attempt to clear.

309

The following day he offered them this prayer that was found scrawled on a piece of wrapping paper in the Ravensbruck concentration camp:

"Lord, remember not only the men and women of good will but all those of ill will. Do not only remember all the suffering they have subjected us to. Remember the fruits we brought forth thanks to this suffering—our comradeship, our loyalty, our humility, our courage and generosity, the greatness of heart that all of this inspired. And when they come to judgment, let all these fruits we have borne be their reward and their forgiveness."

310

Someone asked the Master why he seemed so wary of religion. Wasn't religion the finest thing humanity possessed?

The Master's reply was enigmatic: "The best and the worst—that's what you get from religion."

"Why the worst?"

"Because people mostly pick up enough religion to hate but not enough to love."

311

A disciple put it to the Master point-blank one day: "Have you attained holiness?"

"How should I know?" was the reply.

"Who would know, if you didn't?"

Said the Master, "Ask a normal person if he is normal, and he will assure you he is. Ask a crazy person if he is normal, and he will assure you he is!"

And with that, he gave a mischievous laugh.

Later he said, "If you realize you're crazy, you're not so crazy after all, are you? If you suspect you're holy, you're not so holy after all, are you? Holiness is always unself-conscious."

312

On voting day, the Master would always be the first to show up at the polling booth.

He could never understand why some of the disciples failed to exercise their right to vote.

"People are ready to pay their taxes and shed their blood for democracy," he said. "Why will they not take the trouble to vote and make it work?"

313

A dissatisfied newcomer said to one of the disciples, "I really must know if the Master is holy or not."

"Why should it matter?" said the disciple.

"Why should I follow him if he himself has not arrived at holiness?"

"And why should you follow him if he has? According to the Master, the day you follow someone, you cease to follow truth."

Then he added, "Sinners often speak the truth. And saints have led people astray. Examine what is said, not the one who says it."

314

One of the evil effects of religion, according to the Master, is that it has split humanity into sects.

He loved to tell of the little boy who asked his girlfriend, "Are you a Presbyterian?"

"No," said the little one loftily. "We belong to another abomination!"

315

When asked why seeing was so difficult, this is the story the Master told:

When Sam returned from Europe, his partner in Men's Underwear Ltd., asked him eagerly, "Were you able to visit Rome, Sam?"

"Yes, of course!"

"And did you see the pope?"

"See the pope? I had a private audience with him."

"You don't say!" exclaimed his partner in wide-eyed wonder. "What's he like?"

"Oh, I'd say he's a size thirteen," said Sam.

316

When a group of pilgrims complained that the Master had offended their religious sentiments, he laughingly explained that what he had really hurt was their ego.

And he told them of a bishop who declared the Madonna of the Shrine to be the patroness of the diocese; whereupon all the devotees of the Madonna of the Temple who had unsuccessfully lobbied to have the honor conferred on their own candidate marched in protest and declared a one-day fast in reparation to the Madonna of the Temple.

"Was it the Madonna who was offended or their so-called religious sentiments?" asked the Master.

317

A philosopher who couldn't quite grasp what the Master meant by "awareness" asked him to define it.

"It cannot be defined."

"Is it thought?"

"Not concepts and reflections," said the Master, "but the kind of thought you exercise in moments of great danger when your brain stops dead. Or in moments of great inspiration."

"And what kind of thinking is that?"

"Thinking with your body-brain-being," said the Master.

318

Said the Master, "There are those who think that problems are solved through effort. These people merely succeed in keeping themselves and others busy.

"Problems are only solved through awareness. In fact, where there is awareness, problems do not arise."

319

The preacher was on a tour to various foreign countries.

Said the disciples, "Do you think travel will broaden his mind?"

"No," said the Master. "It will merely spread his narrow-mindedness over a wider area."

320

The Master laughed at people who set themselves up as spiritual guides for others when they themselves were lost and confused.

He loved to tell of the author of *A Guide for Pedestrians* who was run over by a car the day the book was released.

321

When a dictator came to power, the Master was arrested in the act of distributing leaflets at the street corner in defiance of censorship regulations.

At headquarters, his knapsack proved to contain nothing more harmful than blank sheets of paper.

"What does this mean?" the police demanded.

The Master smiled and replied, "The people know what it means."

This story became well known throughout the country, so the local priests weren't one bit amused when, years later, the Master was found distributing blank sheets of paper within the temple precincts.

322

The Master clearly advocated "thought-free," "knowledge-less" contemplation as a means to know Reality.

"How can one *know* Reality without *knowledge*?" a disciple asked.

"The way one knows music," said the Master.

323

A millionaire came to the monastery vowing he would "teach the old fool something of the pleasures of the world so that he doesn't waste his life in the deprivations of a monastery."

The disciples, knowing as they did the Master's delight in the good things of life, laughed aloud when they heard this.

"Teaching the old fool how to enjoy life," said one of them, "would be like giving a fish a bath."

324

The Master was asked, "How does one find God in action?"

He replied, "By loving the action wholeheartedly, regardless of the fruit it brings."

325

To illustrate this for his puzzled disciples, he told them of a man who bought a painting for a million dollars, then framed the canceled check.

"What he really loved was not art," said the Master, "but status."

326

"Is it possible to see the divine?"

"You are seeing it right now."

"Why do we not recognize it?"

"Because you distort it by means of thought."

When they failed to comprehend, the Master said, "When the cold winds blow, water turns into hardened blocks called ice.

"When thought intervenes, Reality is fragmented into a million hardened pieces called 'things.'"

327

"Speak to us about sex."

"Sex," said the Master, "for those who know it, is divine."

"Those who know it?"

Said the Master, "The frog sits next to the flowers quite unconscious of the honey found by the bee."

328

"What is the greatest obstacle to truth?"

"A reluctance to face the facts," said the Master.

By way of illustration, he told of the overweight man who stepped off the scale and said, "According to this height-weight table here, I should be about six inches taller."

Later he told of a woman who finally got around to doing something about her weight: she gave up stepping on the scale!

329

To all firm believers—whether their beliefs were religious, political, or economic—the Master had this message: What you need is not sincerity, but the daring of the gambler; not solid ground to stand on, but the dexterity of the swimmer.

330

One clear, starry night the Master gave his disciples the benefit of his studies in astronomy.

"That is the Spiral Galaxy of Andromeda," he said. "It is as large as our Milky Way. It sends out rays of light that, at a speed of 186,000 miles a second, take 2.5 million years to get to us. It consists of 100,000 million suns, many larger than our own sun."

Then, after a moment's silence, he said with a grin, "Now that we have put ourselves into perspective, let's go to bed."

331

"I seek the peace that comes from death to the self."

"Who is it that seeks this peace?" asked the Master.

"I."

"Now how will your 'I' ever get a peace that will come alive only when your 'I' has died?"

332

Later the Master told the following tale:

When the old dealer in buttons and ribbons died, he left, to everyone's surprise, an enormous fortune in insurance policies.

This, however, did not console his widow, who wailed, "My poor, poor husband. All his life he labored day and night in dire poverty. And now that God has sent us this fortune, he's not here to enjoy it!"

333

The Master once quoted the celebrated words of the Bhagavad Gita in which the Lord urges the devotee to plunge into the thick of battle, while maintaining a peaceful heart at the lotus feet of the Lord.

A disciple asked, "How can I achieve that?"

Said the Master, "Decide to be satisfied with any results your efforts may bring."

334

To explain that what most people seek is not the joy of awareness and activity but the comfort of love and approval, the Master told of his youngest daughter, who demanded that he read from a book of fairy tales before she went to sleep each night.

One day he hit upon the idea of tape-recording the stories. The little girl learned to manage the recorder. All went well for some days till one evening she thrust the storybook at her father.

"Now, darling," said the Master, "you know how to turn on the recorder."

"Yes," was the reply, "but I can't sit on its lap."

335

When a visitor announced he was leaving because he couldn't take another word the Master said, an older disciple was sympathetic.

"I know how you must feel," he said. "For years I avoided the man because his words were like crates that shipped rampaging wild beasts straight from the jungle into my tidy little garden. I would much, much rather have gone to preachers whose words shipped neat white bones from one graveyard to another."

336

The Master chided a disciple who was forever landing himself in trouble because of his compulsion to tell the truth.

"But mustn't we always tell the truth?" the man protested.

"Ah no! The truth is sometimes best withheld."

337

The Master told of a mother-in-law who had come for a week and stayed for a month.

The young couple finally hit upon a plan to rid themselves of the woman. "I'll serve soup tonight," said the wife to her husband, "and we'll start arguing. You claim it has too much salt, and I'll say it doesn't have enough. If Mother agrees with you, I'll get mad and order her out. If she agrees with me, you get furious and order her to leave."

Soup was served. The fight became vicious, and the wife said, "Mother, how about it? Is the soup too salty or not?"

The crusty old lady dipped her spoon into the soup, lifted it to her lips, tasted it carefully, paused for a moment's thought, and said, "Suits me."

338

When a disciple declared his intention of becoming a preacher, the Master wouldn't hear of it. All he said was, "Wait. You are not ready."

A year went by, then two, then five, then ten, and still the Master held on to his prohibition.

One day the disciple said, "Couldn't I do a little good even though I am not ready?"

Said the Master, "How effective will a hunter be who shoots before he has a bullet in his gun?"

339

To explain why holiness is unself-conscious, the Master told of an alcoholic friend who had sworn he would never drink again. One day, suffering from pangs of thirst, he asked the bartender for a lemonade. While it was being prepared, he whispered, "And could you put a little whisky into it while I'm not looking?"

340

The social activist was eager to change the structures of society.

"Fine," said the Master. "But what we need is not just *action* that will bring about change but *sight* that will bring about love."

"So according to you, changing structures is a waste of time?"

"No, no. Changed structures can protect love; they cannot generate it," said the Master.

341

"The trouble with you," said the Master to the preacher, "is that everything you say is absolutely true—and hollow. Your people seek Reality. All you offer them is words."

When the preacher demanded to know what he meant, the Master said, "You are like the man who received a letter from an installment company: 'Will you kindly send us the full amount you owe us?'

"His reply was prompt and clear: 'The full amount I owe you is fifteen hundred dollars.' "

342

The Master sent a strongly worded protest to the governor about his brutal handling of an antiracism demonstration.

The governor wrote to say that he had only done his duty.

Said the Master, "Each time a stupid man does something he should be ashamed of, he declares it to be his duty."

343

The Master once told of two society matrons. One said to the other, "I met your husband the other day. Heavens, what a brilliant man! I suppose he knows everything."

"Don't be silly," said the other. "He doesn't suspect a thing!"

Said the Master, "That's what the scholar is likely to be: someone who knows everything there is to know about Reality and doesn't even suspect its existence."

344

"Why do you travel so little?" a reporter asked.

"To look into the face of just one person or thing every day of the year and never fail to find something new in it—that is a greater adventure by far than any travel can offer," said the Master.

345

The Master heard a disciple speak disparagingly of the greed and violence of "people out there in the world."

The Master said, "You remind me of the wolf who was going through a virtuous phase. When he saw a cat chasing a mouse, he turned to a fellow wolf and said indignantly, 'Isn't it time someone did something to stop this hooliganism?' "

346

"What is the biggest obstacle to Enlightenment?"

"Ignorance."

"Is there just one type of ignorance or are there many?"

"Many," said the Master. "For instance, your particular brand of ignorance demands that you search for Enlightenment."

347

The Master once told of a woman who asked her dentist for the third time to grind down her denture because it did not fit.

"If I do as you say, I fear the teeth won't fit your mouth," said the dentist.

"Who said anything about my mouth?" exclaimed the irritated woman. "The teeth don't fit in the glass."

And the Master concluded, "Your beliefs may suit your mind, but do they fit the facts?"

348

In his younger days, the Master had left his home in search of wisdom.

His parting words were, "The day I find it, I shall let you know."

Many years later, letting them know seemed quite unimportant. That's when he knew that, unknown to himself, he had indeed found it.

349

Speaking of religious leaders who sought to impress others by their outward behavior and dress, the Master told his disciples this tale:

As a drunkard staggered home, he thought of an ingenious way to conceal his condition from his wife: He would sit in his study and read a book. Who ever heard of a drunk person reading a book?

When his wife demanded to know what he was doing there in the corner of his study, he replied cheerfully, "Reading, my dear."

"You're drunk!" said his wife. "Shut that suitcase and come down to dinner."

350

When the Master remarked on the irrationality of a visitor's beliefs, he replied grandly, "I believe because it is irrational."

"Shouldn't you rather say 'I believe because I am irrational'?" said the Master.

351

"How does one attain happiness?"

"By learning to be content with whatever one gets."

"Then can't one ever desire anything?"

"Yes, one can," said the Master, "provided one has the attitude of an anxious father I once met in a delivery ward. When the nurse said, 'I know you were hoping to get a boy, but it's a baby girl,' the man replied, 'Oh, it doesn't really matter, because I was hoping that it would be a girl if it weren't a boy.'"

352

The Master once overheard a disciple say to a visitor, "I have been honored because while hundreds were sent away, the Master singled me out for acceptance as a disciple."

Later the Master said to him privately, "Let's get one thing clear from the start: If you were chosen rather than the others, it is only because your need is greater than theirs."

353

On the subject of the moral upbringing of children, the Master said, "When I was a teenager, my father warned me about certain places in the city. He said, 'Don't ever go into a nightclub.'

" 'Why not, Father?' said I.

" 'Because you'll see things that you shouldn't.'

"This, of course, aroused my curiosity. And at the first opportunity, I went into a nightclub."

The disciples asked, "Did you see something you shouldn't have?"

"I certainly did," said the Master. "I saw my father."

354

"Aren't you going to wish us a merry Christmas?"

The Master glanced at the calendar, saw it was a Tuesday, and said, "I'd much rather wish you a happy Tuesday."

This offended the Christians in the monastery till the Master explained, "Millions will enjoy not today, but Christmas. So their joy is short-lived. But for those who have learned to enjoy today, every day is Christmas."

355

"My former master taught me to accept birth and death."

"Then what have you come to me for?" asked the Master.

"To learn to accept what lies in between."

356

A disciple was convinced she was selfish, worldly, unspiritual. However, after a week's stay in the monastery, the Master pronounced her spiritually fit and healthy.

"But isn't there *something* I can do to be as spiritual as the other disciples?"

The Master replied with this story:

A man bought a car. After careful computation over six months, he came to the conclusion that he was not getting the high mileage so often attributed to such cars. He took it to a mechanic, who declared it to be in perfect condition.

"But isn't there something I can do to increase its mileage?" said the man.

"Well, yes," said the mechanic. "You can do what most car owners do."

"What's that?"

"Lie about it."

357

When asked what he did for his disciples, the Master said, "What a sculptor does for the statue of a tiger. He takes a block of marble and pounds away at anything that doesn't look like a tiger."

When his disciples later asked what exactly he meant, the Master said, "My task is to hammer away at everything that isn't you—every thought, feeling, attitude, compulsion that adheres to you from your culture and your past."

358

One of the Master's reservations about religious leaders was this: They fostered blind credulity in the faithful to the point that, even when some of them dared to raise a question, it was always within the narrow limits of their belief.

There was once a preacher, he said, who honestly sought to get his people to question what he said. So he told them the story of a decapitated martyr who walked with his head in his hands till he came to a wide river. Then, since the martyr needed both hands for swimming, he put his head into his mouth and swam safely across.

There was a moment of unquestioning silence. Then, to the preacher's delight, one man stood up to question the story. "He couldn't have done that!" he exclaimed.

"Why not?" asked the preacher hopefully.

"Because," said the man, "if he had his head in his mouth, he wouldn't have been able to breathe."

359

"Happiness is a butterfly," said the Master. "Chase it, and it eludes you. Sit down quietly, and it alights upon your shoulder."

"So what do I do to get happiness?"

"Stop pursuing it."

"But is there nothing I can do?"

"You might try sitting down quietly—if you dare!"

360

Like Jesus centuries before him, the Master warned people about religion. Left to itself, religion sanctified blind observance of the law. This is how he put it:

A commanding officer asked some recruits why walnut was used for the butt of a rifle.

"Because it has more resistance," said one.

"Wrong!"

"Because it has more elasticity," said another.

"Wrong again!"

"Perhaps because it has a better shine than other woods," said a third.

"Don't be a fool," said the officer. "Walnut is used because it is required in the regulations."

361

"Do you believe in the existence of God?" asked the fanatical believer.

Said the Master, "I shall answer your question if you answer mine. Is your chair the first one to the left?"

"To the left of what?"

"The existence of what?" said the Master.

362

To show his disciples the absurdity of religious authority that came from any source other than personal worth and competence, the Master told of the worker who went to a matrimonial agency.

"Is this a union shop?" he asked.

"Yes, certainly."

He picked out the picture of a beautiful twenty-five-year-old and said, "I'll take her."

"No, you have to take this lady," said the agency director, showing him the picture of a greying woman of fifty.

"Why do I have to take her?"

"Because she," said the director, "has seniority."

363

"How long does the present last? A minute? A second?"

"Much less and much more," said the Master. "Less, because the moment you focus on it, it's gone.

"More, because if you ever get into it, you will stumble upon the timeless and will know what eternity is."

364

Said the Master, "When you were in the womb, you were silent. Then you were born and began to talk, talk, talk till the day you are laid in your tomb. Then you will once again be silent.

"Capture the silence that was there in the womb and will be there in the tomb and even now underlies this interval of noise called life. That silence is your deepest essence."

365

"What's so original about this man?" asked a visitor. "All he gives you is a hash of stories, proverbs, and sayings from other masters."

A female disciple smiled. She once had a cook, she said, who made the most wonderful hash in the world.

"How on earth do you make it, my dear? You must give me the recipe."

The cook's face glowed with pride. She said, "Well, ma'am, I'll tell yer. Beef's nothin', pepper's nothin', onion's nothin'. But when I throws *myself* into the hash, that's what makes it what it is."

About the Author

Anthony de Mello (1931–1987) is the bestselling author of *Sadhana: A Way to God,* with over a million copies in print. A native and lifelong resident of India, he frequently traveled to Europe and the United States to study and teach. His books have been translated into more than thirty-five languages.

Now Available for the First Time
from Image Books

Contact with God

Nowhere are Anthony de Mello's characteristic warmth and insight more evident than in the series of talks he gave while guiding retreats. Known throughout the world as one of the foremost religious guides, in *Contact with God*, de Mello offers the transcripts from his inspiring lectures for readers going on retreat, as well as suggestions for how to get the most out of the experience.

How to Pray

I want to talk to you tonight about something you have come to this retreat to do. You have come here to pray. So I want to speak about prayer, what it is and how to make it. However, before entering into this topic, let me say something to you about two related topics. The first is the need of the experience of God for an apostle; the second, silence.

The Apostle's Need for an Experience of God

Swami Vivekananda tells somewhere of his first encounter with Ramakrishna. The incident illustrates very well what I want to say on this point. Vivekananda, whose name was then Narendra, was a precocious, somewhat conceited young college student who claimed he was an agnostic. He had heard about the holiness of Ramakrishna, so he went to visit him. He found him squatting on his bed. The conversation went something like this:

Narendra: Do you believe in God, Sir?

Ramakrishna: Yes, I do.

Narendra: Well, I don't. What is it that makes you believe in him? Can you prove to me he exists, Sir?

Ramakrishna: Yes.

Narendra: Why are you so sure you will be able to convince me?

Ramakrishna: Because at this moment I see him more clearly than I see you.

The tone of voice in which those words were said and the expression on Ramakrishna's face overwhelmed Narendra. He was never the same again. Those words changed him completely. That is the way it is with the words and, indeed, the whole being of someone who is in direct touch with God. It is disturbing to be in the presence of those who truthfully make the claim that they can sense God and see him—someone like Moses, of whom Scripture says, "He was resolute, as one who saw the invisible God" (Hebrews 11:27).

This is the whole point of our being apostles. The apostle is not just someone with a message. Apostles are their message. When we point out the way of holiness, people will not look at the direction our finger is pointing in. The first thing they will look at is *us*. This is our greatest apostolic need today—not better planning, better equipment, better surveys, better knowledge of our people, their language, their customs, better conversion techniques (if such things exist at all!), but better human beings; a whole new breed of human beings whose lives are evidently charged with the power and presence of the Holy Spirit.

The Identity Crisis

So many priests and religious are undergoing today what is known as an identity crisis. The priest no longer knows what he is and what he is supposed to be in the modern world. This constitutes a problem, yes. But a crisis? We have, no doubt, to study and reflect so as to come up with a more adequate theological definition of what a priest really is, and I can see the liberating effect this will have for the life and work of many priests. But does this lack of an adequate theological definition have to constitute a *crisis* for a priest?

Is a happily married layperson in a state of personal crisis because we are still in search of an adequate theological definition of marriage (and, for that matter, always shall be, given the richness of different cultures and of spiritual realities and the limitations of the human mind)? True, a better definition and a better understanding of marriage will be a help to our laypersons in their married lives. But in the meantime they are experiencing the reality of marriage even though they are not in possession of its definition. They love their spouses and children and are loved by them; they experience the growth and fulfillment which the joys and pains of married life bring with them. There is no reason to be in a state of crisis.

The Imitation of Christ is very wise when it says, "I had rather experience compunction than be able to define it." May we not say the same of many modern priests who are undergoing their identity crisis? Have they *experienced* the meaning of their priesthood and not just *talked* about it? Are they in love with Christ? Are they full of the Spirit? Do they have the fulfillment that comes from giving the Spirit to others, from bringing Christ into the lives of others? If they have, I don't see how they can be going through an identity crisis any more than the happily married people I spoke of earlier. But in order to experience love for Christ you must first have met Christ. In order to give the Holy Spirit you must have experienced his power in your own life. This is what the retreat is all about. It is not a seminar where we speak about Christ. It is a period of silence when we speak to Christ. The speaking about will come later. Let us meet him first, develop an intimacy with him. Then we will truly have something to talk about.

Silence

This brings me to my second topic. There are few things that help so much for conversing with Christ as silence. The silence I speak of is, obviously, the inner silence of the heart without which the voice of Christ will simply not be heard. This inner silence is very hard to achieve for most of us: close your eyes for a moment and observe what is going on within you. The chances are you will be submerged in a sea of thoughts that you are powerless to stop—talk, talk, talk (for that is what thinking generally is, me talking to myself)—noise, noise, noise: my own inner voice competing with the remembered voices and images of others, all clamoring for my attention. What chances does the subtle voice of God stand in all this din and bustle?

Exterior silence is an enormous help for attaining interior silence. If you cannot bear to observe exterior silence, if, in other words, it is unbearable for you to keep your mouth shut, how will you bear the silence that is interior? How will you keep your inner mouth shut? Your tolerance of silence is a fairly good indicator of your spiritual (and even intellectual and emotional) depth. It is possible that when you shut your mouth the noise inside you will become even louder, your distractions will increase, you will be even less able to pray. This is not caused by silence. The noise was there all along. Silence is only making you aware of it and giving you the opportunity to quiet and master it.

Jesus tells us to shut the door when we go to pray. We are obviously not shutting the rest of the world out of our hearts, for we will take its concerns with us to prayer. But that door must be firmly shut or else the noisy world will come in and drown out the voice of God, chiefly in the early stages when concentration does not come easily to us. And the beginner in prayer needs no less concentration than the beginner in mathematics who cannot work on a complex problem when there is a lot of distracting noise around him. The time will come when students of prayer, like mathematics students, will be so gripped by their subject that no amount of noise will be able to take their minds away from their subject. But in the early stages let them be humble and admit their need for quiet and for silence.

The Saints on Silence

The saints have spoken eloquently of the value of silence. Here are a couple of quotes I picked up from a book of Thomas Merton's. One is from a Syrian monk, Isaac of Nineveh. What he says is as true for the solitary in the desert as for the apostle in the heart of a modern city. He says,

> *Many are continually seeking, but they alone find who remain in continual silence. . . . Every man who delights in a multitude of words, even though he says admirable things, is empty within.*

If you love truth, be a lover of silence. Silence like the sunlight will illuminate you in God and will deliver you from the phantoms of ignorance. Silence will unite you to God himself.... More than all things, love silence: it brings you a fruit that tongue cannot describe. In the beginning, we have to force ourselves to be silent. But then there is born something that draws us to silence. May God give you an experience of this "something" that is born of silence. If only you practice this, untold light will dawn on you in consequence ... after a while a certain sweetness is born in the heart of this exercise and the body is drawn almost by force to remain in silence.

Every word in those lines is worth meditating on. These words will speak powerfully to the heart of anyone who has ever experienced the treasures there are in silence.

The other quote on silence is from a desert Father, Ammonas, a disciple of St. Anthony's:

Behold, my beloved, I have shown you the power of silence, how thoroughly it heals and how fully pleasing it is to God. Wherefore I have written to you to show yourselves strong in this work you have undertaken, so that you may know that it is by silence that the power of God dwelt in them, because of silence that the mysteries of God were known to them.

Isaac of Nineveh is obviously speaking from experience when he says, "In the beginning we have to *force* ourselves to be silent." Silence doesn't come easily to us at the start. When we try to observe it we shall notice strong resistances within us; Eveyln Underhill tells us the value of overcoming these resistances in her book *Mysticism*:

The self is as yet unacquainted with the strange plane of silence which so soon becomes familiar to those who attempt even the lowest activities of the contemplative life; where the self is released from succession, the voices of the world are never heard and the great adventures of the spirit take place.

Adventures, indeed. You will make thrilling discoveries once you have suffered through the initial boredom and restlessness that silence brings. You will find that this dark silence is really filled with heavenly light and with heavenly music; that what at first sight seemed empty and nothingness is really filled with the presence of God. A presence that it is impossible to describe but that is somehow conveyed so attractively in the words of Simone Weil when she tries to describe the effects she felt on reciting the Lord's Prayer:

At times the very first words tear my thoughts from my body and transport it to a place outside space where there is neither perspective nor point of view. . . . At the same time, filling every part of this infinity of infinity, there is a silence, a silence which is not an absence of sound but which is the object of a positive sensation, more positive than that of sound. Noises, if there are any, only reach me after crossing the silence.

After listening to these words, I imagine that you need no further urgings from me to plunge into strict silence these days—for you are not likely to get such a fine opportunity in the rest of the year and the effects of silence are cumulative, that is, the silence that comes after four days of silence is deeper than the silence you have at the start of the retreat.

How to Pray:
Jesus the Master of Prayer

If this retreat is to give you the rich fruit you are expecting of it, you must invest a long time in prayer. And if you are to pray well, you must know how to pray. How are you to pray? This is a question that the apostles asked of Jesus. And Jesus himself taught them what they were to do when they were in prayer. This is fortunate for us, because we too can learn from him how to pray. There is no better master in the art of prayer; in fact, for us Christians, there is no other master.

In Luke 11 we read, "Once, in a certain place, Jesus was at prayer. When he ceased, one of his disciples said, 'Lord, teach us to pray, as John taught his disciples.' " How wise of the apostles to have direct recourse to the Master when they wanted to learn how to pray. I advise you to do the same. No one can teach you to pray, really. I certainly cannot. The conferences I shall be giving you these days will, please God, be something of a help to you in your prayer life. But, sooner or later, you are going to run into difficulties that no earthly teacher will be able to solve for you, and you will have to have direct recourse to Jesus and say to him, "Lord, teach me to pray." And he will solve your difficulties for you and guide you personally. So I advise you, right from the start, whenever you run into difficulties and find the going tough, to look at Jesus and say, "Lord, teach me to pray." Say it again and again—for the whole day if need be. Say it without strain or anxiety, calmly, in the firm expectation that he will teach you; as indeed he will! Here then is the first answer to the question "How to pray?" Go to Jesus and ask him to teach you. That is how you learn to pray.

Printed in the United States
by Baker & Taylor Publisher Services